From Italy with Amore

From Italy with Amore

SEASONAL ITALIAN RECIPES FOR THOSE YOU LOVE

JESSI & ALESSIO PASINI

DK

DK | Penguin Random House

Publisher Mike Sanders
Art & Design Director William Thomas
Editorial Director Ann Barton
Editor Brandon Buechley
Assistant Director of Art & Design Becky Batchelor
Acquisitions Editor Anna Wostenberg
Editorial Assistant Resham Anand
Cover & Lifestyle Photographer Rebecca Denton
Food Photographers Ted Thomas & Elena Craig
Recipe Tester Lovoni Walker
Copyeditor Mira S. Park
Proofreaders West Matuszak & Bianca Bosman
Indexer Beverlee Day

First American Edition, 2026
Published in the United States by DK Publishing
1745 Broadway, 20th Floor, New York, NY 10019

The authorized representative in the EEA is Dorling Kindersley Verlag GmbH. Arnulfstr. 124, 80636 Munich, Germany

26 27 28 29 10 9 8 7 6 5 4 3 2 1
001–354788–AUG2026

A catalog record for this book is available from the Library of Congress.
ISBN 979-8-2171-3255-3

DK books are available at special discounts when purchased in bulk for sales promotions, premiums, fund-raising, or educational use. For details, contact SpecialSales@dk.com

Illustrations © aniok / shutterstock

Printed and bound in China

www.dk.com

FSC MIX Paper | Supporting responsible forestry FSC™ C018179 www.fsc.org

This book was made with Forest Stewardship Council™ certified paper – one small step in DK's commitment to a sustainable future.
Learn more at **www.dk.com/uk/information/sustainability**

for Lorenzo Leone

Contents

Introduction

...

Primavera

Spring

ANTIPASTI E CONTORNI

PIATTI PRINCIPALI

DOLCI

BEVANDE

...

Estate

Summer

ANTIPASTI E CONTORNI

PIATTI PRINCIPALI

DOLCI

BEVANDE

Autunno

Fall

ANTIPASTI E CONTORNI

PIATTI PRINCIPALI

DOLCI

BEVANDE

Inverno

Winter

ANTIPASTI E CONTORNI

PIATTI PRINCIPALI

DOLCI

BEVANDE

Introduction

First things first: If you're here to break spaghetti in half, close the book. Just kidding. (But seriously, we're watching you.)

We're Jessi and Alessio—also known as "The Pasinis," an Italian and American couple who fell in love and built an online community by sharing our relationship, our cultures, and our kitchen. Sure, Jessi broke a few culinary rules along the way (some on purpose, some by accident), but really, who's counting? (Except for Alessio.) Our love of cooking together started right after we began dating, and it was a way for each of us to treat the other to beloved family recipes and cultural dishes. Over the years, we began to craft our own unique recipes based on our travels or as a way to recreate our favorite Italian dishes that we couldn't find in the US. Whether you've been with us from the beginning, laughing along with the pranks and celebrating when Alessio rates something a "10 of the 10," or if you're just here for some great, authentic recipes, this cookbook is our love letter to you and to Italian food that's *actually* Italian.

The title, *From Italy with Amore*, means more than just recipes from Italy. It's a reflection of everything Alessio and I hold dear (tradition, love, and a whole lotta pasta) but also a nod to our own love story. "Amore" means love in Italian, and it's what Alessio has called me since our early days of dating. In a way, the title of this book also reflects that journey: Alessio, coming from Italy, and me, "Amore." Together we're bringing you the recipes, stories, and little moments that have filled our relationship with so much joy.

This book is an invitation. It's our request that you slow down, gather around a table, and cook meals that are simple, seasonal, and satisfying. Whether you're an absolute beginner in the kitchen, or the go-to "pasta person" of your friend group, our goal is to make authentic Italian food feel not only possible, but joyful.

This cookbook isn't *just* about pasta, though (but trust us, there's plenty of it!). It's about the little things that make life beautiful, like teaching your new American girlfriend to salt pasta water after she's spent more than 20 years thinking it was optional. It's about your Italian partner forgiving you for unknowingly feeding him fettuccine Alfredo on the first date. It's about finding recipes you *both* love by experimenting and learning together along the way.

In these pages you'll find recipes that have been passed down through generations and some that were created in our own little kitchen, candles lit, retro Italian love songs playing from the laptop. You'll find seasonal recipes with tips on how to shop like an Italian. (Yes, even in a standard US grocery store.) We'll show you how to buy the right kind of pasta and *why* it's important. We'll help you taste test olive oil like a true sommelier, and we'll teach you how to follow your instincts in the kitchen like the famous Italian Nonnas do. The beauty of this book is that there are recipes for everyone—from easy-to-learn basics, to more challenging, regional specialities. In addition to recipes, each season of this book features a special bonus section. You'll learn things like how to host an unforgettable summer Italian dinner party on page 138 and what to serve at a cozy, traditional Italian Christmas lunch on page 246. Think of this book as a guide, as a coach, and as a stiff side-eye from us when you reach for pre-grated "Parmesan" in a can …

We hope *From Italy with Amore* brings you joy, entertainment, and inspiration, just like our journey together has brought to us. We hope these recipes that have been such a special part of our story will now become a part of *your* story, too. We hope by the end, both your belly and your heart will be full.

With tanto amore,

Jessi & Alessio

What Makes Italian Food So Delicious

What makes Italian food so delicious? It's simple. Literally.

• • •

Let's be honest: Italian food has no business being this good with so few ingredients. How is it that a plate of spaghetti with garlic, olive oil, and a couple Italian chili peppers can bring someone to actual tears? It's not a trick. It's not luck. It's a philosophy. One that says, "Buy good ingredients, don't mess them up, and whatever you do, don't rush."

Italian food doesn't thrive on being complex. In fact, the beauty is in the simplicity of the ingredients. Let a perfect tomato shine by pairing it with a bit of salt and a drizzle of extra virgin olive oil. Treat that wedge of Parmigiano Reggiano like the treasure it is and savor it. Give your pasta just enough sauce to coat, not drown. It's about respecting ingredients, tradition, and time. In doing so, you'll learn that the "classic" recipes are classics for a reason.

1. Ingredients come first. Always.

If it's not good on its own, it's not going in the pot. Italian cooking isn't about hiding flaws. In fact, Alessio says if a dish is overcomplicated, it's usually hiding something—low-quality ingredients. Great Italian food begins at the market. Sure, you can find "supermarkets" around Italy, but the real magic is shopping the traditional way. Going to the bakery for bread, the cheese shop for cheese, buying fresh, local vegetables at the Monday farmer's market. When someone has taken the time to devote all of their energy to creating one product for you to buy, you know it's going to be good. Many times, it's so good it doesn't need anything else. Whether it's the ripest tomato or the right kind of olive oil, the ingredients do the heavy lifting. You're just there to put them in the right place. The Italian motto? Don't overdo it—just do it right.

Takeaway: Buy the best ingredients you can afford. Then get out of their way.

2. Eating seasonally is a way of life.

Zucchini blossoms in summer. Chestnuts in autumn. Citrus in winter. Strawberries in spring. Italians cook with what's in season not to be fashionable, but because that's when things taste best. If you hate raw tomatoes, chances are you're eating those sad, mealy, watery ones and not the one picked fresh from a summer garden. The ones that taste robust and like they've been kissed by the golden sun. Italians swear by eating seasonally because again, a great dish starts with great ingredients, and you won't find ingredients any better than when they're at the peak of the growing season. The rhythm and vibe of the year makes its way to the plate.

Takeaway: If it's in season, it's in the kitchen. If it's not, we wait. Trust us, the waiting makes it that much more delicious when it's finally time to indulge.

3. Tradition + technique = magic

Recipes are passed down like sacred spells—one generation to the next. Everyone's Nonna makes the best sauce, and you know what? It's probably true! Italians value the traditional way of cooking, spending time with family, and not rushing things. But there's also technique: Knowing when to salt the water, how to emulsify a sauce, and why you don't need to rinse your pasta. Italian food is less about following strict measurements, and more about learning the feel of things. Cooking with your eye and heart rather than your head. If you're lucky enough to have someone share their secret family recipe with you, it probably doesn't include quantities or detailed instructions. "Go by eye" is a popular saying among Italian home cooks. It's a tricky talent to learn, but once you get the hang of it, it becomes second nature.

Takeaway: Trust tradition—but taste everything. Italians don't measure, they vibe. But we also value a good kitchen scale when you're just starting out!

4. Balance is everything.

Italian dishes have an elegance in how they balance fat, acid, texture, and freshness. A rich carbonara is cut by a sprinkle of black pepper and sharp Pecorino. A tangy tomato can be mellowed by sweet, creamy burrata. Every bite has contrast—and harmony.

Takeaway: Each ingredient plays its part. Build contrast, not chaos. Be intentional about what you're putting on the plate.

5. Mealtime is sacred.

Italian food tastes better because it's rarely rushed. This is something Alessio has had to teach me … I'm always in a rush while he's perfectly happy to let a sauce develop for 3 hours on the stovetop. In Italy, meals are shared. Tables are set. Wine is poured. Conversation flows. This respect for the process of cooking and eating somehow makes the food taste more alive.

Takeaway: Learn to slow down. We know it's not easy, but you've got to try. If you're not smiling while you cook, you're not doing it right.

Kitchen Tools

. . .

Before we dive into the recipes, let's talk tools. Because it loves to be simple, Italian cooking doesn't require a kitchen full of the latest gadgets. A good wooden spoon, a sharp knife, and a solid stainless steel pot will take you further than the fanciest countertop appliance that you only use "once in a while." The following items are the ones we reach for every day. We keep it very easy in our kitchen and we recommend you do, too. Think of this list as your "Italian kitchen starter pack"—it's reliable, timeless, and practical.

Everyday essentials

These are your ride-or-die tools.

- **Large Pasta Pot** Pasta needs room to move, and you need space so that you're not tempted to break the spaghetti in half so it fits in the pot. Get one big, nice pot and it'll be all you use.
- **Large Skillet or Sauté Pan** For sauces, sautéing vegetables, and finishing pasta. We usually don't worry about different sizes (small, medium, large). We have one large sauté pan and use it for almost everything. It's important to note that a sauté pan has more depth and a straight side compared with the more shallow and sloped skillet. You might find one works better than the other for a specific recipe.
- **Small Saucepan** For warming sauces, making syrups, or heating milk.
- **Wooden Spoons** Alessio swears they work better than all the others. We have a nice collection that we've gathered over the years, but you really only need a few: a good stirring spoon, a slotted spoon, a spatula, and a ladle. Yes, all of these tools are wooden in our house.
- **Chef's Knife** One sharp knife does more than a drawer full of dull ones. We use the same knife almost every single day.
- **Cutting Board** A large, sturdy surface you can actually use. When we finally splurged on a good one, it made a world of difference. No more sliding around while kneading pizza dough and no more shaking when chopping vegetables.
- **Microplane or Box Grater** For cheese and zest. We have one of each: one box grater that we use to grate our cheese and one microplane for zesting fruit. It's important to note that when grating hard cheese for garnish, you should use the smallest holes on your box grater! If the pieces are too big, the flavor of the cheese can overpower the dish. It's most traditional to use the smallest holes that look like little metal "stars." The cheese should look like snow as it falls to the dish. When grating cheese for melting, use the larger holes.
- **Colander** A must for draining pasta. Just remember to check whether you need to reserve any pasta water for the sauce first.
- **Fine-Mesh Strainer** Our go-to for draining off small bits from broth or juice. We also use it to dust our baked goods with powdered sugar or our tiramisù with cocoa powder.

Baking & pasta add-ons

These aren't necessary for your first spaghetti alla carbonara, but if you're diving deep into homemade doughs, desserts, or anything pastry-adjacent, you'll want these:

- **Food Processor** For pie crusts, fillings, and quick doughs. However, your hands and a little elbow grease can do the job just fine. We've ground down nuts and basil for pesto and made a simple pie crust from butter and flour without one and it's been absolutely fine.
- **Dutch Oven** My must-have tool for baking the perfect loaf of bread. It's also great for roasts and soups. However, before we saved up to buy our first, we baked and cooked without one for years.
- **Pasta Roller** For making pasta from scratch. You can definitely hand roll pasta sheets, too, but this gives you the perfect smooth texture and even thickness.
- **Electric Mixer** A countertop stand mixer is lovely, but it's also expensive and takes up a lot of space. We find an electric mixer gets the job done just as well. Whichever one you have in your kitchen is perfect for cakes, whipped cream, stiff egg whites, and anything fluffy.

- **Mortar & Pestle** For real-deal pesto, spice grinding, and for those very "ancient apothecary vibes." You'll feel really cool when you get your first one. It doesn't have to be huge. We have a small marble one that we use all the time.
- **Rolling Pin** Essential for pasta, pastry, and cookies. Don't tell Alessio, but I prefer the "French" rolling pin because I feel I have more control over the dough.
- **Round Cake Pans (8-inch/20 cm or 9-inch/23cm)** We recommend at least two tucked in the cabinet. If you're feeling really fancy, add a Bundt pan into the mix, too.
- **Lasagna Pan/Casserole Dish (9 × 13-inch/ 23 × 33cm)** For lasagna, pasta bakes, and mixed veggies.
- **Sheet Pans** For roasting vegetables and baking the perfect conventional oven pizza. We have two 12 × 16-inch (30 x 41cm) ones and we use them so much that they've developed an amazing patina. They're clearly well loved.

Nice-to-haves

aka, if you're really committed or just love a gadget

- **Mandoline** For slicing zucchini paper-thin. Just please use the hand guard. Full transparency, we got one of these but returned it because it was scary. We kept feeling like we would cut ourselves, so now we stick with a sharp knife instead.
- **Espresso Maker or Moka Pot** Not essential for cooking (unless you want the perfect espresso for your tiramisù!) but essential for life. Alessio bought me my first one when I was spending tons of money on coffee shop drinks every morning. It saved me a lot of money, and yes, it 100% tastes better. This is a must-have for Italians.
- **Digital Scale** Of course, optional, but we highly recommend it. We use it to measure the correct grams of pasta for each serving and weigh our pizza dough for precision. It steps up your cooking game with accurate measurements.
- **Bench Scraper** For dividing dough, scooping up herbs, and looking very professional while doing these things.
- **Tongs** For tossing pasta or salad or flipping veggies and meats while cooking. However, we think a couple of forks can work just fine.

Hard pass

- **Garlic Press** Smash it with your knife like nature intended.
- **Electric Can Opener** Unless you're opening 500 cans of tomatoes a week.
- **Single-Use Tools (egg separators, avocado slicers, apple corers, etc.)** Unless it sparks serious joy, skip it.
- **A Million Knives** Again, one good knife beats twelve mediocre ones. You don't need to spend your money on a fancy set. We use the same knife every day. Just keep it nice and sharp and you'll be good to go.

Our most loved tools and brands

- **Made In Stainless Steel Pots** We use these every single day. Yes, like all high-quality cookware, they are an investment, but for us, it's absolutely worth the splurge if you can swing it. You can avoid toxic chemicals leaching into your food, and you'll be able to cook soup, pasta, and sauce like a professional chef.
- **Wooden Spoons (especially olive wood, maple wood, and the ones we inherited from my grandmother)** Okay, technically she wasn't Italian—but Alessio loved her and gave her honorary citizenship. Her spoons are still going strong, stirring sauces, making memories, and infusing our food with years of love.
- **Bialetti Moka Pot** No espresso machine? No problem. This classic, stovetop coffee maker produces a strong, rich espresso that feels just like Italy and tastes just like home for Alessio.
- **Stainless Steel Everything** We're a stainless steel household. It's cleaner, sturdier, healthier, and very satisfying to cook with. We're talking stainless steel baking sheets, box graters, mixing bowls, you name it. If it's your first time switching over from nonstick cookware, it can take some getting used to. There's a bit of a learning curve in how to heat it and clean it properly, but after a few sauces, you'll get the hang of it.

Sourcing Authentic Italian Ingredients (and Substitutions) in the US

Because not everyone has a Nonna mailing them Pecorino Romano fresh from Sardinia.

. . .

One of the trickiest parts of cooking Italian food in the US isn't learning the techniques—it's finding the right ingredients. This is especially true if you're not living in a major city.

There's a big difference between actually Italian and "Italian-ish," and grocery store aisles are full of imposters wearing red, white, and green to try and pull you in. But don't panic. You don't need a Tuscan vineyard or a Roman street market. You just need a little guidance and a solid sense of what's worth hunting down, what's worth splurging on, and what you can confidently swap. It may not be perfect, but it'll get you as close as can be.

We'll help you decode the labels, find the good stuff, and know when a substitution will still get Alessio's seal of approval. Are you ready to bring a little bit of Italy to your pantry?

Note: We love supporting small Italian grocery stores and specialty markets when we can, but here are some big-name stores that often surprise us and have just what we're looking for: Publix, Whole Foods, Eataly, Sprouts, World Market, Fresh Market, and online Italian import stores like Supermarket Italy and Gustiamo.

Olive oil: The soul of the Italian Kitchen

If there's one ingredient to splurge on, let it be the olive oil. A high-quality extra virgin olive oil adds richness, fruitiness, and depth, whether you're drizzling it over grilled vegetables, pasta, or soup. Bonus points from Alessio if you're giving your bread a quick dip, too!

But more than that, good olive oil is packed with health benefits that cheap oils just can't compete with. Those benefits come from "polyphenols"—natural antioxidants that help reduce inflammation and protect heart health. That $5 grocery store bottle? It might technically be olive oil, but chances are it's been sitting on a shelf too long, it's low in nutrients, and tastes flat or even rancid. The worst thing is that olive oil can actually oxidize and lose all of its beneficial antioxidants. It's important to seek out quality olive oil that is processed well, shipped properly, and stored properly. Yes, the price tag might be higher, but you're getting real flavor and real nutrition. You're also ensuring the workers who harvested and produced the olive oil are making a living wage.

What to look for

- "Extra virgin" on the label. Ideally, it should also be organic.
- A harvest or best-by date (fresher is always better). In case you didn't realize it, olive oil does go bad. Typical recommendations are that high-quality olive oil lasts 30 to 60 days after opening.
- A dark glass bottle. (Light can degrade the olive oil's flavor, aroma, and health benefits.)
- 100% from one region—whether it's Italy, Spain, Greece, California, or elsewhere. What matters most is that it's not a blend of oils from different countries. You want olives grown, pressed, and bottled all in the same place. Consistency = quality.
- Bonus points if it's from a small producer or has traceability information on the label.

Our go-to brand? Entimio. Their oils are single-origin, organic, high in polythenols, and consistently win gold medals at the World Olive Oil Competition.

If you can't splurge on everything in this book, we get it. But if you're going to invest in one thing, let it be this. Almost every recipe in this book uses extra virgin olive oil, and if you're consuming something so often, it's important for it to be high-quality. Your sauces, salads, and soups, and your health, will thank you.

Pasta: Trust us, it matters.

Dry pasta is totally traditional—just make sure you're buying the good stuff. Especially if you eat as much pasta as we do. A high-quality pasta not only tastes better and holds sauce beautifully, it's actually better for your health. Yes, we're serious.

Most industrial pasta is dried at super high temperatures to save time and money, but that shortcut creates furosine, a compound that forms when heat damages the pasta's proteins. High furosine levels means fewer nutrients, poor digestibility, and a less pleasant texture. Traditional pasta, like the kind made the "old-fashioned" way, is dried slowly at low temperatures (around 113°F/45°C, but up to 140°F/60°C is acceptable) for up to 72 hours. This process, although time-consuming, helps preserve nutrients and gives the pasta its iconic chew.

You can even see the difference. Cheap pasta is bright yellow and very smooth. This is from the high-heat drying. The good pasta? Its pale, ivory hue tells you it was made with care in mind, not speed.

What to look for

- 100% durum wheat semolina.
- Bronze-cut (look for a rough texture on the pasta that clings to the sauce).
- Small-batch, artisanal producers.
- A light, matte, ivory color, not shiny or bright yellow.
- Be wary of sales gimmicks like "lenta lavorazione" or "slow-worked" on the packaging. You have no guarantee of the time and temperature if a brand doesn't explicitly list it on the packaging.)

Our favorite brand? Afeltra. It's made in Gragnano, the pasta capital of Italy. It checks every box: light ivory color, slow-dried at low temperatures (both temp and time listed specifically on the packaging), bronze-cut, and delicious in every dish.

Cheese: No green cans. Ever.

If you learn just one thing from this cookbook, let it be this: Parmigiano Reggiano is not the same as Parmesan. Not even close. It's like comparing a symphony orchestra to a doorbell.

Most Americans grow up with the green can version, or maybe later in life, upgrade to a wedge of Parmesan, but those are often domestic imitations with muted flavors and a completely different aging process. Parmigiano Reggiano, on the other hand, is made in specific regions of Italy under strict DOP (Denominazione di Origine Protetta/Protected Designation of Origin) regulations and aged for 12 to 36 months (or longer). The result is nutty, savory, crystalline, and layered with depth.

When I first tasted real Parmigiano Reggiano, after years of eating store-bought and canned Parmesan, I felt like I had been lied to my whole life. I didn't even know cheese could taste like that. It was slightly sharp but very creamy, with those tiny crunchy crystals. (By the way, they're amino acid crystals, not salt!) It was melt-in-your-mouth delicious and left a warm, savory, almost brothy aftertaste. It didn't just top the pasta. It transformed it.

And how do you know you're getting the real deal? Look for the name Parmigiano Reggiano stamped into the rind. That's the sign you're about to taste something truly special.

Authentic picks

- Parmigiano Reggiano: Nutty, salty, deep. Look for the DOP seal and rind stamp.
- Pecorino Romano: A bold sheep's milk cheese with sharp saltiness. Perfect for cacio e pepe and carbonara.
- Fresh Mozzarella: Soft, milky, and packaged in water or whey. Look for "fior di latte" (cow's milk) or "di bufala" (buffalo milk). We recommend the brand BUF when shopping in a traditional grocery store.
- Ricotta: Choose whole milk ricotta made with simple ingredients. Sheep's milk ricotta is even more traditional if you can get it.

What to look for

- Check the ingredient list. Milk, rennet, and salt are really all you need.
- Avoid additives. If it sounds like a chemistry equation, it's not real Italian cheese.
- Country of origin matters. Look for DOP/IGP certifications.
- Packaging clues. Don't be fooled by an Italian flag on the front. Do a bit of digging and really read the label.
- Watch the mozzarella. Good mozzarella often comes water-packed, not shredded.

Tomatoes: Canned, jarred, and what to actually buy

San Marzano tomatoes are the gold standard. They're sweet, low-acid, and grown in volcanic soil near Naples. They give sauces a magical quality. But even if you're not using DOP San Marzanos every time, it's important to know what to look for and what to skip in the grocery aisle.

When it comes to tomato products, we always prefer glass jars over cans whenever possible. Glass protects flavor and quality better than metal, especially for passata (pureed tomatoes), which is one of our favorite pantry staples. That said, there are still some amazing canned options, and yes—we absolutely keep Cento and Mutti in our pantry, too.

The biggest trap in the US when it comes to tomatoes is the wall of jarred pasta sauces and "pizza sauces." These are usually overly seasoned, too sweet, and so heavy that they completely drown out the taste of the tomato. Alessio always says the number one thing to look for in a sauce is that it actually tastes like tomato. If it needs basil, garlic, or salt, you can add it yourself. Keep it simple and let the tomato shine.

What to look for

- Whole peeled San Marzano. DOP-certified, if possible.
- Passata in glass jars. Smooth tomato puree, great for fast sauces.
- Brands we love: Mutti and Cento.
- A short ingredient list. Just tomatoes, maybe basil. That's it. None of the extra stuff.

A note on tomato paste, "conserva": In Italy, tomato paste is called conserva, and it's rich, thick, and full of concentrated tomato flavor. We love using it to deepen a sauce, but just a spoonful goes a long way. Look for it in a tube rather than a can—it's easier to store and usually better quality.

Herbs and extras: Fresh is best

but dried has its moments, too

Herbs can transform a dish, but knowing when to use fresh versus dry can be confusing. The flavor, texture, and even the way they're added to a dish can totally shift the result.

Fresh herbs bring brightness and a variety of different aromas. They're best added at the end of cooking or sprinkled on just before serving. Dry herbs are more concentrated and slightly earthier, and need heat to reawaken their flavors. Add them early in the cooking process so they can soften and release their oils. You also want to make sure to use a bit less at first and taste. Because they are strong, you might not need as much as you think.

We typically use fresh herbs, but there are absolutely moments when dry is the way to go.

Herb tips

- Basil: Always fresh, always added last.
- Oregano: Dry is absolutely okay. Rub it between your fingers to bring out the oils before adding.
- Parsley: Use flat-leaf, not curly. Fresh adds color and a soft lift. Italians love this stuff and use it in so many dishes.
- Thyme and rosemary: We typically use fresh, but we've been known to use dry in a pinch. If using dry, note that it is more potent, so go light.
- Sage: Use fresh, especially when infusing butter. Dry can be too harsh.
- Mint: Fresh only, unless you're making tea.

Thinking about an herb garden? You don't need a huge backyard or a fancy setup. A sunny window or a few pots on the porch is all it takes. We started our herb garden with basil, oregano, rosemary, parsley, thyme, and mint. Herbs are easy to grow and endlessly useful. There's something extra joyful about stepping out to the garden, scissors in hand, to snip some fresh herbs for a recipe.

How to keep herbs fresher, longer

Soft herbs (parsley, basil, cilantro): Trim the stems and place them in a glass of water like a bouquet. Cover loosely and store in the fridge (except basil—keep it on the counter, away from cold).

Hard herbs (rosemary, thyme, sage): Wrap in a damp paper towel, place in a reusable bag or container, and store in the fridge crisper drawer. They'll last a week or more this way.

Capers, anchovies, and olives

These are secret weapons in the kitchen. Look for versions packed in brine or olive oil, not vinegar. They bring a saltiness and depth to a recipe that no dry herb ever could.

Seasonal Ingredients

Cook like you're grabbing straight from the garden.

. . .

The secret to Italian cooking? It tastes good because the ingredients are good. And ingredients taste good when they're at their freshest. In Italy, meals are built around what's fresh and abundant at the market. They don't cook with out-of-season produce. They wait. I can't tell you how many times we've scoured a restaurant menu trying to find one of our favorite dishes, only to be told by the waiter, "Sorry, it just went out of season." When a fruit or vegetable season finally does come around, Italians go wild for it and use it in as many recipes as they can. That's why so many trattorias offer seasonal menus that change as the months go by. They know this is the best way to give their customers high-quality, great-tasting food.

This section gives you a seasonal cheat sheet to help you cook like Italians do: in rhythm with the year. Not only does it make your food taste better—it makes cooking feel more alive. You don't have to be a farmer's market regular to make these recipes work. But if you're standing in the produce aisle wondering what to reach for … this list has your back. Snap a pic of it on your phone and always keep it with you.

Spring (March–May)

- Artichokes
- Asparagus
- Baby broccoli
- Carrots
- Cherries (starting late spring)
- Fava beans
- Fresh herbs (parsley, mint, basil; starting late spring)
- Leeks (early spring)
- Lemons
- Peas
- Radishes
- Ramps
- Spinach
- Spring onions
- Strawberries

Summer (June–August)

- Apricots (late spring, early summer)
- Bell peppers
- Cherries (early summer)
- Corn
- Cucumbers
- Eggplants
- Figs (late summer)
- Fresh basil
- Garlic (cured heads)
- Green beans
- Melons (cantaloupe, honeydew)
- Oregano
- Peaches
- Plums
- Tomatoes (all kinds!)
- Watermelon
- Wild berries (blueberries, blackberries, raspberries)
- Zucchini and zucchini flowers

Autumn (September–November)

- Acorn squash
- Apples
- Broccoli rabe
- Brussels sprouts
- Butternut squash
- Cabbage
- Chestnuts
- Fennel (arrives in late fall, peaks in winter)
- Grapes
- Mushrooms
- Pears
- Pumpkin
- Radicchio
- Rosemary
- Sage
- Swiss chard
- Walnuts

Winter (December–February)

- Bay leaves
- Beets
- Broccoli
- Cabbage
- Carrots
- Cauliflower
- Celery root
- Chicory
- Citrus (oranges, lemons, mandarins, blood oranges)
- Fennel
- Kale
- Leeks
- Pomegranates (late fall to early winter)
- Potatoes
- Thyme
- Turnips

Italian Cheeses

What makes them so great!

. . .

Italian cheese could be the subject of a book all on its own. Salty, creamy, smoky, sharp, nutty, fresh, aged—the options are abundant. In Italy, you'll find cheese melted into baked pasta, grated or shaved over risotto, or eaten straight off the block in chunks with bread and wine. Unfortunately, because these cheeses are so good, they're often imitated but never quite replicated. Once you taste the real stuff, you can never go back.

One of the things we love about Italian cheese is how it fits with intention into the food culture. It's not included in a recipe just to be indulgent—it serves a purpose. Pecorino Romano adds sharpness; Parmigiano Reggiano adds depth; fresh, creamy burrata cools. Even a sprinkle of ricotta salata on top of a dish can add the perfect salty finish.

There are more than 400 varieties of cheese in Italy (at least), but you'll see the same core handful pop up in traditional recipes again and again. And if you're going to splurge on something special for a recipe, let it be the cheese. Look for names like "DOP" (Denominazione di Origine Protetta/ Protected Designation of Origin), which means it was made in the traditional way, in the region it's meant to come from. And if you're not sure what to buy? Ask your cheesemonger for a taste. Trust your tongue. It'll know.

For now, let's walk through the key cheese players and what makes them the perfect addition to your dish.

Parmigiano Reggiano

The king of cheeses. This is a cheese that makes Alessio cry from happiness.

What makes it great

- Aged 12–36+ months (the older the better, in our opinion).
- Hard, nutty, salty, and full of delightfully crunchy amino acid crystals.
- Grate it over almost anything (pasta, risotto, soup, vegetables, ice cream … okay maybe not ice cream, but you get the idea).
- Can be eaten all by itself as a snack.

How to buy it & storage tip

- Look for the rind stamped with "Parmigiano Reggiano" and make note of the DOP mark. DOP signifies that it is made in the provinces of Parma, Reggio Emilia, Modena, Bologna to the left of the Reno River, and Mantua to the right of the Po River.
- Depending on the flavor profile of what you want, get a younger or older cheese. For a more mild and sweet taste, look for 12–18 months aged; 24 months aged is a blend of sweet and savory; and 36 months aged is the most savory, bold, and intense.
- Buy wedges of the cheese whenever you can and grate it yourself.
- Cheese paper or parchment paper wrapping is best as it allows the cheese to breathe and provides the right level of humidity.

Pecorino Romano

The cheese that melted our hearts the first time we had real carbonara in Rome.

What makes it great

- Salty, sharp, and made with sheep's milk.
- It stands up to bold flavors. That's why it's perfect in a dish like cacio e pepe, which features a lot of intense black pepper. It's also the ideal ingredient to cut through the creamy egg and salty guanciale in carbonara.
- It's sharper than Parmigiano Reggiano, which is great when you want a cheese that's more "in your face" (in a good way, of course).
- It grates so beautifully. You'll have to buy some and try it for yourself to see what we're really talking about.

How to buy it

- Look for the DOP mark to make sure it's coming from the correct Italian regions (Sardinia, Lazio, and the province of Grosseto in Tuscany) and was made using traditional methods.
- Look at the color. It should be creamy white compared with the more golden tones of Parmigiano Reggiano.

Mozzarella di bufala

Creamy and milky. No matter if it comes from buffalo or cow's milk, mozzarella is delicious. However, most people in Italy agree, mozzarella made from buffalo milk is top of the line.

What makes it great

- The buffalo milk version of mozzarella is creamier and tangy.
- It's best eaten fresh, not cooked. Drizzle it with olive oil, layer it in caprese, or add it to the top of your pizza after cooking.

How to buy it & storage tip

- Never shredded in a bag—never. Always look for it submerged in liquid.
- It shouldn't be tough or rubbery.
- When cut, it should release a soft, flowy, and milky center.
- Always keep it in its liquid before consuming.

Ricotta

Fluffy and mild. A cheese for comfort.

What makes it great

- Ricotta is actually made from whey, which is a substance left over from the production of other cheeses. It can be made from sheep, cow, goat, or buffalo milks.
- Ricotta in Italian means "re-cooked." It comes from the process of making ricotta after already using the milk to make a different cheese.
- It's used in both savory and sweet recipes: everything from pasta and pizza to pastries, cakes, and ice cream.
- Sheep's milk ricotta is the traditional gold standard for cannoli filling.

How to buy it

- Look for as few ingredients as possible to make sure you're getting the best-quality product.
- Nowadays, cow's milk ricotta is most common. However, if you want to add an unexpected element to cannoli or other dishes, try sheep's milk instead.

Mascarpone

It's kind of like Italian cream cheese, only silker and more elegant.

What makes it great

- It's a key ingredient in tiramisù, aka the best dessert ever invented.
- It can be folded into whipped cream, used as frosting, added into recipes for creaminess, or spread on top of bruschetta.
- It has a milky, buttery flavor with no tanginess.

How to buy it

- Look for a simple ingredient list. The best mascarpone is traditionally made with only fresh cream and a gentle acid like lemon juice. However, modern methods commonly use citric acid as well.
- Buy imported mascarpone when possible. Italian-made mascarpone is incredibly rich in flavor and smooth in texture.
- The texture should always be creamy and never have separation or curdling.

Gorgonzola

Italy's version of blue cheese.

What makes it great

- It comes in two styles: "dolce," which is sweet and creamy, and "piccante," which is stronger and crumbly.
- It adds a distinctive bite to a dish or sauce.
- We love it in pasta or risotto because it keeps an otherwise regular cheese sauce from being "boring."

How to buy it

- Know which type you need for your recipe before buying. Dolce or piccante add completely different flavor profiles to a dish.

- Check the rind. Authentic Gorgonzola should have a slightly sticky rind and blue veins running through the interior.
- DOP matters here again. To be authentic Gorgonzola, it must be produced in the Northern Italian regions of Piedmont and Lombardy.

Honorable mentions

- **Taleggio** A semi-soft, washed-rind cheese. It has a strong smell but a buttery taste.
- **Provolone** A sharp, firm cheese that's great for melting.
- **Scamorza** A Southern Italian, stretched-curd, cow's milk cheese. It gets its pear shape while it's hanging to dry. It can also be smoked for a lovely flavor.
- **Fontina** Dreamy, cow's milk cheese that melts to perfection.

Alessio's regional spotlight

Friuli-Venezia Giulia's hidden cheese gems

Italy's most world-famous cheeses might come from other regions, but if you head north to the Alpine-meets-Adriatic region of Friuli-Venezia Giulia, where Alessio is from, you'll find some truly special, lesser-known cheeses that we think deserve a little highlight.

- **Montasio** Alessio's all-time favorite cheese. The first record of Montasio comes from more than 250 years ago. According to those documents, Montasio was considered a high-quality product at the time, priced much higher than other cheeses. The production techniques for Montasio date to 13th-century Benedictine monks. It has now become the identity of the region, even acting as the base for its most famous dish: frico friulano. It's a semi-hard cheese with a buttery flavor, perfect for melting into various dishes or snacking on its own.
- **Formai del Cit** A spreadable cow's milk cheese that's traditionally stored in stone jars called "cit" in the local dialect. It started as a way to use up leftover or imperfectly blended cheeses. It's made from mixing Latteria and Montasio cheeses of various ages, adding milk, and blending by hand to form a thick cream. It's left to rest for several hours before being ground up with peppercorns and added to the jars. It's so good I can eat it with a spoon.
- **Jamar cheese** Also known as cave cheese, it's made from raw cow's milk that's left to age for months in humid karst caves. It has a rough, moldy, brown rind, but underneath it's crumbly, with strong, earthy, and nutty flavors.
- **Formadi Frant** This is another cheese created out of the desire to reduce waste. It was traditionally made from other cheeses with defects so they wouldn't have to be thrown out. It's made by breaking up three or four cheeses of various ages; adding salt, pepper, and sometimes other spices; and blending with milk or cream. It's placed in a mold and left to age. It's another favorite of ours.
- **Malga** This is a cheese made from a blend of cow's milk and goat's milk. It's left to age on wooden boards for several months or up to a year. It's a semi-hard cheese with a soft yellow color and irregular holes. Its flavor is mostly sweet with a slight bitter accent, grassy, and pleasant due to the alpine flowers and herbs that the cows graze on.

Can you find these cheeses in the US? Occasionally … however, it's often very tricky. If you have an Italian specialty shop near you that features some Northern regional products, ask them if they can source any of these cheeses. If not, there might be ways to order online. Otherwise, a trip to Friuli might be in your future!

How to Taste for Good Olive Oil

. . .

In Italian cooking, olive oil isn't just something you occasionally take out of the pantry to drizzle on pasta or toss in a salad. It's one of the most important ingredients that should always be in your kitchen. It's not uncommon to taste olive oil like you would wine, swirling it in a glass like a true, professional sommelier.

Alessio and I learned how to properly taste olive oil from one of our friends who just happens to actually be a real olive oil sommelier. Once we learned the proper techniques, we were surprised by how complex the oil truly is. Good olive oil has layers. Its flavors range from grassy and peppery to floral. It should make your throat tingle a bit when you try it, and it should always have a bitterness rather than a smooth or buttery finish. The bite signals quality, freshness, and loads of beneficial polyphenols. If your olive oil doesn't have it, it suggests a low quality, or a blended oil, or worse—rancidity.

To properly taste olive oil, pour a small amount into a little glass or spoon. True sommeliers traditionally use blue glasses so they aren't influenced by the color of the oil. Take the glass and swirl it between the palms of your hands for a couple of minutes to warm it. Inhale and note what you smell. It should be light and fresh. If something smells "off" or spoiled, that's a bad sign.

Take a small sip (less than a teaspoon) and let it coat your tongue. Then, with your teeth closed but lips slightly open, draw a short breath of air in through your mouth (strippaggio), bringing the air and olive oil into the back of your palate. It should spread across your tongue and tingle in the back of your throat. Be careful not to gulp or swallow. You should instead be taking a controlled, tasting breath. This is called "aerating" and allows more of the oil flavors to be released into all spaces of the mouth. Do you taste green apples? What about almonds, grasses, artichokes, tomatoes? Fruitiness or pepperiness? These are all signs of great olive oil. If it tastes flat, greasy, or stale, it probably is. A great olive oil is often more bitter than what you may be used to. Think about eating an olive straight from the tree. It would be so bitter that you'd most likely spit it out. They don't taste smooth and buttery like jarred olives. The same goes for dark chocolate vs milk chocolate. The health benefits and higher polyphenols of dark chocolate make it taste more bitter. Remember this when you're tasting olive oil.

We recommend extra virgin, cold-pressed, and a single, traceable origin. The bottle it comes in should be a dark glass to protect it from light. It should have a harvest date and origin listed. It's also ideal if the top of the bottle only has a small hole to pour through rather than a large mouth, in order to prevent oxidation.

With olive oil, you absolutely get what you pay for. You don't have to buy the priciest bottle on the shelf, but keep in mind that the higher price tag signifies quality, traceability, tested health benefits, and certified organic status, and it means that the farm where the oil is produced is most likely paying the workers a living wage. Among the many mass olive oil manufacturers, this is often not the case.

The last tip is this: Olive oil absolutely has an expiration date. We were surprised to know that a lot of our followers were keeping the same bottle of olive oil in their kitchen for years and years. Olive oil 100% goes bad. Certain things can speed up the oxidation and, unfortunately, damage the polyphenols, antioxidants, and other healthy aspects of the oil. Time, light, heat, and oxygen are the enemies of olive oil. After opening a bottle, you should consume it within 30 to 60 days.

In short, monitor the expiration date of your olive oil, keep it away from light and heat, and minimize oxidation.

Italian Cooking Tips

Never break the pasta! (And when to break the rules!)

...

If you've ever cooked with an Italian (or married one), you probably already know there are a lot of rules. Rules. Not suggestions. These are sacred, Nonna-approved, centuries-old rules, and despite what you might have heard, Italians didn't create these rules just to be stubborn or superior. They exist for a reason. They help preserve flavor, texture, tradition, and health. Once you understand why they matter, you'll also earn the right to bend them, sometimes ...

Never break the pasta.

The why: Long pasta shapes like spaghetti, linguine, bucatini, etc. are designed for twirling. If Italians wanted a short pasta in the dish, they'd reach for something else like rigatoni, fusilli, or penne. Breaking long noodles ruins the experience and the texture.

When to break this rule: Never. Get a bigger pot or find patience to gently push the noodles down into the water as they soften and cook. The only, only exception to this rule is soup. Sometimes you can break pasta into tiny pieces for soup (or for your kids).

Salt your pasta water like the sea.

The why: Alessio was truly horrified to learn I had never salted my pasta water before we started dating. This is a crucial step in cooking. It's your only opportunity to season the pasta itself. Salty water adds a hint of flavor. Otherwise, the dish will fall flat. I just didn't know any better, but now I do.

When to break this rule: If you're on a low-sodium diet or wanting something super mild for kids. Otherwise, salt it.

Cheese and seafood don't mix.

The why: The delicate flavor of seafood can be overwhelmed by sharp cheeses. If they're eating a seafood dish, Italians want to actually taste the fish.

When to break this rule: Never. There are plenty of recipes in Italy that mix seafood with cream sauces, though. Just not cheese. If you absolutely, positively have to have cheese on your seafood, do us a favor and don't tell us. Also, keep it as mild as possible.

Pasta must be al dente.

The why: In Italian, "al dente" means "to the tooth." It gives texture and bite to the dish, prevents mushiness, and helps hold the sauce. It's also considered to be better in nutritional value and for digestion.

When to break this rule: To be honest, we're always breaking this rule. We cook our pasta a minute past "al dente" to "cotto." It's still firm but has a softer bite than al dente. Just be careful because there's a specific line in pasta cooking that's easy to cross. Never, ever let it get mushy or gummy. That old tradition in the US that says, "if the pasta sticks when it's thrown on the wall, it means it's done" is wrong. That's definitely an overcooked noodle.

Don't rinse your pasta.

The why: The starch helps the sauce cling to the pasta. Rinsing removes it and cools the pasta unnecessarily.

When to break this rule: If you're in a hurry to cool pasta down when making pasta salad. Otherwise, leave the starch where it is.

No cappuccino after 11:00am.

The why: In Italy, cappuccino is considered a breakfast drink. It's also believed that milk after a meal messes with digestion.

When to break this rule: This is actually a rule that's softening in Italy, and Alessio agrees. Sometimes an afternoon cappuccino is cozy and delicious. Just don't break one cardinal rule: Never, ever, ever drink a cappuccino with a meal. We've seen people drinking cappuccino alongside their pasta or pizza. This is just an absolute no.

Tomato sauce doesn't need a lot of sugar or garlic.

The why: For some reason there's this myth that Italian food is supposed to be super garlicky. This couldn't be further from the truth. Italians believe you can easily overdo the garlic. In fact, they often put a clove in while something is cooking, only to remove it right before serving. They only want the essence of garlic. You can also overdo the sugar. It dulls the brightness of good, fresh tomatoes. We actually don't put any sugar in our sauce. Instead, if we want to balance the acidity, we might throw a carrot in while the sauce cooks. The natural sugars balance the acids and then we remove the carrot at the end.

When to break this rule: Never. So many jarred sauces outside of Italy overdo it on sugar, garlic, and spices. You are meant to taste the tomato in the sauce. Don't cover up the flavor with unnecessary additions.

Grate cheese the right way.

The why: In Italy, Parmigiano Reggiano and other cheese garnishes are meant to enhance a dish, not bury it. That's why Alessio always recommends using the smallest "star-like" holes on a box grater in order to make the cheese look like fine, powdery snow. Anything bigger and you risk changing the texture or throwing off the balance of flavors in a dish. Despite what you might be used to, too much cheese can actually ruin a dish, masking the taste of a sauce. Microplanes and shredding holes might look fancy or feel easier to handle, but they make pieces that are too large. The goal is to create light, delicate cheese that adds a gentle touch of its flavor.

When to break this rule: If the cheese is melting into a dish, like in a baked pasta or a creamy sauce, you can use larger holes. But for finishing a dish, always aim for the fine "cheese snow."

There are of course hundreds of other rules that pop up when discussing Italian cuisine; however, the most important rule is: "cook with love." The spirit of Italian cooking isn't meant to be rigid. It's meant to be alive, flavorful, and celebratory of simple ingredients and traditions passed from kitchen to kitchen.

Primavera

Spring

antipasti e contorni

Insalata di Fave

Fava Bean Salad

• • •

4 servings

This bright, fresh salad is springtime in a bowl. In Italy, fava beans and Pecorino Romano are often eaten together around Easter, especially in regions where both come into season at the same time. It's simple: buttery fava beans and sharp cheese. We've taken a classic combo and tossed it in a little lemon, olive oil, and some toasted pine nuts to create a dish that tastes rustic but is right at home on an elegant family dining table.

We won't lie, the first time you see it, you might say, "That's it?" But as soon as you take a bite, you'll understand. It's the perfect flavor for when the sun finally comes out, the windows are open, and you're enjoying the slow pace of the world coming to life again. It's also the perfect excuse to use up fava beans if you see them at the market and aren't sure what to do with them. Just promise us you'll use *real* Pecorino Romano. When something is so simple, the ingredients you use make all the difference.

1½ tbsp pine nuts

3 cups (360 g) fresh, shelled fava beans

1 oz (28 g) shaved Pecorino Romano, plus more for serving

For the dressing:

2 tbsp extra virgin olive oil

1 tbsp lemon juice

Zest of ½ lemon

1 garlic clove, minced

Sea salt and pepper, to taste

1. Toast the pine nuts in a small skillet over medium-low heat until golden brown, 3 to 5 minutes. Set aside.
2. Bring a large pot of salted water to a boil.
3. Add the fava beans and cook for 1 to 2 minutes, or until the beans are floating and tender.
4. Drain the beans, rinse under cold water, and set them aside. Doing this allows you to easily remove the second shell, if desired; however, the beans are still delicious without removing this skin.
5. *To make the dressing:* In a medium bowl, whisk together all the dressing ingredients.
6. Toss the beans in the dressing until well combined. Add the Pecorino Romano and pine nuts and toss again.
7. Transfer to a serving dish and top with extra Pecorino Romano.

antipasti e contorni

Asparagi al Forno

Oven-Roasted Asparagus

• • •

4 servings

This is one of those dishes that shows up on our table almost weekly once spring arrives. It's simple, quick to make, and so good we sometimes find ourselves snacking on pieces straight from the baking sheet. It's our go-to side to pair with a simple grilled chicken breast and Alessio's yummy Patate in Padella (Pan-Fried Potatoes, page 39). With only a few ingredients, it's proof that sometimes the best food is the least fussy. It's also an easy way to add some seasonal vegetables to your table. Good, quality ingredients shine here and don't need a lot to make them taste delicious. A dusting of Parmigiano Reggiano brings everything together, making this a spring favorite we return to again and again.

1 lb (454 g) fresh asparagus
2 tbsp extra virgin olive oil
1 garlic clove, minced
Sea salt and pepper, to taste
1 oz (28 g) finely grated Parmigiano Reggiano
2 sprigs fresh thyme

1. Preheat the oven to 350°F (180°C).
2. To prepare the asparagus, first wash them thoroughly and trim off the tough white bottoms.
3. Place the asparagus on a baking sheet, drizzle with the olive oil, and use your hands to toss so that each piece of asparagus is fully coated. Make sure the stems aren't overlapping.
4. Season with garlic, salt, and pepper. Sprinkle with the Parmigiano Reggiano.
5. Place the thyme sprigs on top and bake for about 20 minutes, or until completely cooked. (The asparagus should be tender and easily pierced with a fork.) Thin or thick asparagus will have different cooking times, so adjust accordingly.
6. Remove the thyme sprigs and serve as a side dish alongside your favorite main.

antipasti e contorni

Patate in Padella

Pan-Fried Potatoes

• • •

2 servings

This is Alessio's signature side dish, and I honestly can't count the number of times we've eaten it. It's simple, satisfying, and totally addictive—a win-win in our book. Sometimes we make a whole meal out of it, pairing it with arugula salad and fresh chunks of Parmigiano Reggiano. Other times, it's the perfect companion to grilled chicken or even homemade cheeseburgers (*Gasp!* Yes, Alessio *does* like American food despite what you might've been told.)

Once you've had these potatoes, crisped in olive oil with garlic and rosemary, you'll have a hard time eating potatoes any other way. And if you have fresh rosemary growing in the garden, even better.

- 1 lb (454 g) medium yellow potatoes
- 2 to 3 tbsp extra virgin olive oil
- 2 garlic cloves, unpeeled
- 1 sprig of fresh rosemary, stem removed and leaves chopped
- Sea salt, to taste
- 1 tsp unsalted butter (optional)

1. Clean, scrub, and thoroughly dry the potatoes. Slice each potato lengthwise into quarters and then slice each quarter into even sections, about ⅛ inch (3mm) thick.
2. Heat the olive oil in a large frying pan over medium-low heat. Add the potatoes and garlic to the pan.
3. Cook the potatoes, allowing them to develop a crisp crust on each side, flipping them occasionally to prevent sticking or burning.
4. After 15 minutes, add the chopped rosemary. Cook for an additional 3 minutes, until the potatoes are golden brown on all sides.
5. Season with salt.
6. Optional secret ingredient: After the potatoes are finished, you can remove the pan from the heat and melt in 1 teaspoon of butter. Rotate the pan so that the butter is evenly dispersed, allow to cool slightly, and serve. The potatoes become even more crispy as they cool.

antipasti e contorni

Bruschette Stagionali

Seasonal Bruschetta

• • •

6 to 8 servings per season

Let's settle something right away: It's "broo-SKET-tah," not "broo-SHET-tah." If you say it wrong again, prepare to get the "Italian hand" from Alessio. The word *bruschetta* comes from the Roman dialect verb *bruscare*, which means "to toast." The essence of bruschetta is simply toasted bread. However, there can be many variations. Drizzle it with olive oil or rub it with garlic and top it with whatever is in season. It's a simple, versatile crowd-pleaser.

This recipe celebrates that versatility with a year-round approach. One vibrant bruschetta for each season, starting, of course, with the season you're currently reading: spring. For this season, you'll snack on fava beans and burrata. In the summer, juicy tomatoes. In the fall? Figs and prosciutto. Winter rounds things out with smoked salmon and ricotta. Whether you serve these as an appetizer, a light lunch, or as part of a cozy dinner party spread, these bruschette are the perfect way to make the most of seasonal ingredients.

• • •

1 loaf of artisan bread with a strong crust and crumb, about 4 to 5 inches (10 to 13 cm) wide (no baguettes!)

Extra virgin olive oil

Sea salt and pepper, to taste

1. Preheat the oven to 350°F (180°C).
2. Cut the bread into ½-inch (1.25 cm) slices. Place them on a parchment-lined baking sheet and drizzle with olive oil.
3. Season with salt and pepper and bake for 8 to 10 minutes, until crisp and golden. Remove from the oven, set aside, and allow to cool completely.

• • •

For Spring:

1 large carrot

3 medium radishes

2 tbsp extra virgin olive oil

4 mint leaves

1 cup (120 g) fresh shelled fava beans

Sea salt and pepper, to taste

12 oz (340 g) burrata

½ cup (36 g) microgreens

1. Wash and peel the carrot and finely grate it with a box grater.
2. Wash the radishes and slice them into thin rounds.
3. Add the olive oil to a small bowl. Tear the mint leaves by hand and add them to the bowl. Add in the grated carrot, radish slices, fava beans, and salt and pepper, to taste. Mix to coat the vegetables.
4. Assemble the bruschetta by spreading a tablespoon of burrata onto each of the bread slices. Garnish with the vegetables and a bit of microgreens and serve on a platter.

For Summer:

2 cups (420 g) cherry tomatoes

2 garlic cloves

Pinch of sea salt

8 small basil leaves, plus more for garnish

Extra virgin olive oil

1. Wash and dry the tomatoes. Chop them into small ¼-inch (6 mm) pieces.
2. Peel the garlic cloves and mince one, setting the other aside.
3. Combine the tomatoes, the minced garlic, and salt in a small bowl. Cover with a plate and let it rest for 30 minutes.
4. When you're ready to assemble, take the other peeled garlic clove and rub it on each bread slice.
5. Roughly chop the basil and add it to the bowl of tomatoes, along with a drizzle of olive oil. Stir to combine.
6. Spoon some of the tomato mixture onto each bread slice, and drizzle with a bit of the liquid in the bowl. Garnish with a basil leaf and serve on a platter.

For Fall:

2 tbsp diced chives
7 oz (200 g) Gorgonzola dolce
Sea salt and pepper
8 to 10 fresh figs
16 pieces of prosciutto crudo
Acacia honey

1 Rinse and finely chop the chives. Place them in a small bowl and add the Gorgonzola and a bit of salt and pepper. Mix to combine and set aside.
2 Clean and dry the figs. Slice each of them into 6 pieces of equal size.
3 Spoon some of the Gorgonzola mixture onto each bread slice. Top with one or two pieces of prosciutto. Arrange a few fig slices over each. Drizzle with honey and serve on a platter.

For Winter:

6 oz (170 g) ricotta, drained
½ cup (120 g) plain Greek yogurt
Pinch of sea salt and pepper
7 oz (200 g) smoked salmon, thin slices
Fresh dill

1 Combine the ricotta, Greek yogurt, and a pinch of salt and pepper in a small bowl.
2 Cut the salmon into thin, bite-size strips, about ¼- to ½ inch (3 mm to 1.25 cm) wide.
3 Spoon some of the ricotta mixture onto each piece of bread and top with the sliced salmon.
4 Sprinkle with a garnish of hand-torn dill and serve on a platter.

antipasti e contorni

Sformato di Carciofi

Artichoke Flan

. . .

4 servings

I might be addicted to this dish. I often find a version of it listed as an "antipasto" when we're out at a restaurant in Italy, and as soon as I spot it on the menu, my mouth begins to water. To be honest, it might sound a bit odd by name, but artichoke flan is something truly special—creamy, delicate, and full of earthy flavors.

In Italy, especially in Rome and throughout the central and southern regions, artichokes are a staple of springtime. They're celebrated everywhere from street food to fine dining, and you often see them piled high on market stalls. This dish is one of our favorite ways to highlight their flavor. It feels elegant but humble, and it's often served as an appetizer—though I could make a meal of it with a slice of crusty bread dipped in olive oil.

- 6 fresh artichokes
- Juice of 1 lemon
- 2 large yellow potatoes
- ½ cup (120 ml) heavy cream
- 2 large eggs, lightly beaten
- 2 oz (57 g) freshly grated Parmigiano Reggiano, plus more for serving
- ¼ tsp ground nutmeg
- 1 tsp sea salt
- Pepper, to taste
- 1 to 2 tbsp unsalted butter
- ½ cup (60 g) plain dry breadcrumbs

Special Equipment

- Blender or food processor
- Four 8-oz (240 ml) oven-safe molds or ramekins

1. Clean the artichokes. Remove and discard the stems, tough outer leaves, chokes, and thorny tips, leaving only the heart and soft, tender inner leaves. (See Note.) Chop each artichoke into four small pieces of equal size.
2. Add the lemon juice to a large bowl of cold water, and soak the artichoke pieces until you are ready to cook them. This will prevent them from browning.
3. Peel and chop the potatoes into 1-inch (2.5 cm) pieces.
4. Bring a stock pot of water to a boil over high heat. Transfer the artichokes from the lemon water to the stock pot. Add the potatoes to the stock pot. Lower the heat to medium and cook the artichokes and potatoes until soft, 10 to 15 minutes, testing with a fork to make sure they are tender.
5. Drain the artichokes and potatoes, rinse in cold water, and then blend in a blender or food processor until smooth.
6. Preheat the oven to 350°F (180°C).
7. Combine the artichoke mixture, heavy cream, eggs, Parmigiano Reggiano, nutmeg, salt, and pepper in a large bowl.
8. Grease the molds generously with the butter. Use the breadcrumbs to line the bottom and side of each mold.
9. Fill each mold three-quarters full with the artichoke mixture. Bake for 25 to 30 minutes, until golden and firm. Let stand for 10 minutes before serving.
10. Turn out the contents of each mold onto a plate and sprinkle with additional Parmigiano Reggiano.

NOTE

Use a sharp knife to cut off the top half of the leaves and most of the stem. Carefully use your hands to peel off the tough outer leaves, being wary of the thorns. With a paring knife, cut/shave off the remaining hard, darker green peel until you get to the soft inner portion that is lighter in color. Cut the heart in half and scoop out the choke with a spoon or paring knife. Only the heart and the soft inner leaves should remain.

antipasti e contorni

Focaccia Genovese

Genoa-Style Focaccia

. . .

6 servings

We could make a whole meal out of focaccia. In fact, this was our go-to beach lunch when we were on our honeymoon: a couple of fresh focaccias and a few ripe peaches picked up from the market on the way. It was simple, exactly what you want when the sun is shining, and your only plan is to stay in place and nap by the sea.

This version comes from Liguria, a crescent-shaped coastline in the northwestern corner of Italy, bordering the Ligurian Sea. It is thinner and more delicate than the taller, fluffier focaccias you'll find in places like Puglia, aka, the heel of Italy's boot. The inside is soft, the bottom is crisp, and the top is perfectly golden and salty. Warning: It's so good, it never survives more than a few hours.

- 3⅓ cups (400 g) all-purpose flour, plus more for sprinkling
- 2 cups (250 g) Manitoba flour
- 1½ cups (360 ml) warm water
- 2 tbsp (10 g) diastatic malt powder
- 2 tsp sea salt
- 2¼ tsp (7 g) active dry yeast
- 2 tbsp extra virgin olive oil, plus more for greasing and topping
- Brine (2 tsp salt dissolved in ½ cup/240 ml water)

Special Equipment

- Wooden spoon
- Two 12 × 16-inch (30 × 40 cm) baking sheets
- Rolling pin (optional)

1. In a large bowl, whisk together the flours. Press the center down to make a well and pour in the water. Mix together with a wooden spoon to roughly combine.
2. Mix in the malt powder, salt, and yeast, to combine into a loose dough.
3. Transfer the dough to a lightly floured work surface and knead for 5 to 10 minutes, until the dough is smooth and elastic.
4. Pour the olive oil over the top of the dough and continue to knead until the oil is absorbed, adding a small amount of flour if the surface is too sticky. Be careful not to add too much. Knead for about 15 minutes in total.
5. Cover the dough with a damp kitchen towel and let it rest for 10 minutes.
6. Divide the dough into two equal pieces. Shape one piece into a rectangle about ½ inch (1.25 cm) thick. Fold the rectangle like you would fold a piece of paper to fit into an envelope, one side folded in and then the other folded over the top. Repeat with the second half of the dough. Cover both with a damp kitchen towel and let rest in a warm place for 30 minutes.
7. Grease each baking sheet with 1 tablespoon of olive oil.
8. Transfer one rectangle of dough to a baking sheet and use your fingers to gently press down and spread until it covers the area of the baking sheet. Repeat with the second rectangle. Take special care not to handle the dough too roughly or break the developing air bubbles that are necessary for the perfect focaccia.
9. Cover with damp kitchen towels and let the dough rectangles rest for 30 minutes in a warm place.
10. Using your fingertips, gently press the dough into the edges of the baking sheet, making a little ridge along each side. Make sure all edges are sealed up with the dough, as you do not want the brine to leak under the dough when it is poured over. Cover again with damp kitchen towels and let rest for 1 hour.

NOTE

As you get comfortable with this recipe, feel free to experiment with adding toppings such as rosemary, olives, or cherry tomatoes.

11 Uncover the sheets of dough and sprinkle a small amount of all-purpose flour over the top. Using your fingers, very gently push into the dough to make the famous holes, about ½ inch (1.25 cm) apart. Again, do not use too much force and release the air bubbles.

12 Pour 2 tablespoons of olive oil and half of the brine in the center of each focaccia. Spread it gently with your hands to fill all the holes. Take care not to let the brine leak under the focaccia dough. Let rest for another hour, uncovered.

13 While the dough is resting, preheat the oven to 450°F (230°C).

14 Bake the focaccia for about 20 minutes, until golden brown and crispy on the bottom. You can check by gently lifting the corner of the focaccia with a spatula.

15 Cool slightly before slicing and serving. (See Note.)

piatti principali

Zuppa di Pollo e Verdure

Chicken Soup

• • •

4 servings

Alessio and I get so excited when the flowers start to bloom and the birds begin to sing, but early spring still brings the occasional cold snap. That's when this soup swoops in to save the day. It's warm, nourishing, and exactly what you want when you're craving comfort. Alessio makes it often, especially when one of us is under the weather. On days when one of us isn't feeling our best, this soup is like a warm hug in a bowl. I've watched him make this so many times now, and every step is done with care. He never rushes. He lets everything cook as long as it needs to because it's that consideration and patience that finds its way into the food and makes it taste *that good.* The rich, golden broth (full of simple, nourishing ingredients) is delicious enough to sip on its own, but we also love using the leftovers in dishes like Risotto agli Asparagi (Asparagus Risotto, page 48) or Tortellini in Brodo (Tortellini in Broth, page 210).

This recipe is a cornerstone of our kitchen. It's a recipe that's never quite measured exactly, but somehow always turns out just right.

Sea salt

1 whole chicken (approximately 3½ lbs/1.5 kg), giblets removed

1 white onion

4 medium orange carrots

2 celery stalks

Extra virgin olive oil

1 Heat a large stock pot full of water over medium-high heat until just boiling. Heavily salt the water and put in the whole chicken, adding additional water if needed, so that the chicken is fully submerged.

2 Lower the heat to medium, cover, and cook for 1 hour, skimming off the fat throughout.

3 Meanwhile, peel off the outer layer of the onion, clean and peel the carrots, and clean and peel the celery. You can halve the carrots and celery if you feel they won't fit into your pot.

4 After the chicken has cooked for 1 hour, add the whole vegetables into the pot and cook for another hour, continuing to skim off the fat as needed.

5 Remove the chicken and vegetables. You can strain the broth if desired, but we usually don't.

6 Chop the chicken and vegetables into bite-size pieces.

7 Spoon the broth into a bowl and add some of the chicken and vegetables. (See Note.) Finish with a drizzle of olive oil before serving.

NOTE

Leftover broth can be used for risotto, soup, tortellini, etc.

piatti principali

Risotto agli Asparagi

Asparagus Risotto

• • •

2 servings

This is one of Alessio's go-to risotto recipes, and let me tell you why: It's simple, it's seasonal, and the ingredients are easy to find here in the US. We love making risotto together, but some of our favorites, like our beloved Risotto Salsiccia e Radicchio (Sausage and Radicchio Risotto, page 163), can be tricky to replicate outside of Italy. The sausage just isn't the same.

But asparagus? It's beautiful in the spring, and this risotto captures its freshness while lovingly blending it into creamy goodness. It's a dish that's elegant enough to serve at a dinner party but comforting enough to make on a casual evening at home. When risotto hits that perfect, creamy consistency, it transports us right to our favorite trattoria in Alessio's hometown.

2 tbsp extra virgin olive oil

½ yellow onion, diced

¾ cup (150 g) dry arborio rice

2 to 2½ cups (480 to 600 ml) prepared vegetable broth (either from scratch, premade, or from a bouillon cube), plus more as needed

1 lb (454 g) asparagus

½ oz (14 g) grated Parmigiano Reggiano

2 tsp unsalted butter

Sea salt and black pepper, to taste

Special Equipment

Immersion blender

1. Heat the olive oil in a large sauté pan over medium-low heat. Add the onion and cook for 5 to 7 minutes, until golden and translucen.
2. Add the rice and toast it for 1 to 2 minutes, stirring to prevent burning.
3. Ladle 1 to 1½ cups (240 to 360 ml) of broth into the pan and lower the heat to medium-low for a simmer.
4. Wash and prepare the asparagus by removing the tough white bottoms. Cut the stalks into 1 inch (2.5 cm) pieces.
5. Add about three-quarters of the chopped asparagus into the pan with the rice and broth.
6. Combine the remaining asparagus with 1 cup (240 ml) of broth in a separate medium bowl, and use an immersion blender to blend until smooth. Add this mixture into the pan.
7. Let the rice cook, adding more broth little by little when it gets too dry. Be careful not to add too much broth too quickly or you risk overcooking the rice while waiting for everything to evaporate. Cook the risotto in this manner for 15 to 16 minutes, until the rice is tender with a slight bite.
8. Once the rice is cooked and any extra broth has evaporated, remove from the heat.
9. Stir in the Parmigiano Reggiano and butter until smooth and creamy. Add salt and pepper, to taste.

piatti principali

Risi e Bisi

Italian Rice and Peas

. . .

4 servings

This classic dish from the Veneto region sits somewhere between a risotto and a soup. Traditionally eaten on April 25th to celebrate the Feast of San Marco in Venice, it's a celebration of spring's earliest green peas. We love it not only for its history, but also for its delicious flavor. Don't be fooled by the luscious texture. There isn't any heavy cream in there. Instead, the richness comes from blending the pea pods into a silky broth and stirring with patience to allow the perfect texture of rice to develop. It features the power couple of Italian cooking: simplicity and seasonality.

- 2 lbs (907 g) fresh peas in the pod
- 4 cups (1 L) vegetable broth
- 2 tbsp extra virgin olive oil
- 1 yellow onion, diced
- 1¾ cups (350 g) dry rice (traditionally Vialone Nano, but arborio or carnaroli are okay, too)
- 2 oz (57 g) finely grated Parmigiano Reggiano
- 4 tbsp unsalted butter
- 1 tbsp chopped fresh parsley
- Sea salt and pepper, to taste

Special Equipment

Immersion blender

1. Clean the pea pods thoroughly and then remove the peas from the pods. Rinse the empty pods under cold water.
2. Add the broth and pea pods to a large stock pot and cook partially covered over medium heat for 1 hour.
3. Remove from the heat and allow to cool slightly before using an immersion blender to blend and combine the pods and the broth until smooth.
4. Heat the olive oil in a large sauté pan over medium heat. Cook the onion for 5 to 7 minutes, until golden and translucent. Be careful not to burn the onion.
5. Add in the fresh peas, stir, and cook for 2 to 3 minutes, until they begin to soften.
6. Add in the rice and toast it for 2 to 3 minutes, until translucent. Stir to prevent burning.
7. Add the pea pod mixture to the pan and bring to a boil. Reduce the heat to medium-low and simmer for about 15 to 16 minutes, until the rice is cooked. Stir continuously during this process so the rice cooks evenly and doesn't burn.
8. Once the rice is cooked, turn off the heat. Stir in the Parmigiano Reggiano, butter, parsley, salt, and pepper, and mix everything until smooth and creamy.

piatti principali

Frittata Primavera

Spring Vegetable Frittata

• • •

2 servings

When Alessio and I first started dating, we had a minor cultural clash over eggs. I was used to seeing them at the breakfast table, but Alessio was *horrified*. In Italy, eggs (especially frittata) are usually a lunch dish. And I, in turn, was completely thrown off when he suggested we eat eggs in the middle of the afternoon.

Eventually, we each won the other over, and Alessio came to appreciate a nice plate of bacon, eggs, and hash browns, while I developed a love for frittata with a side of salad. Frittata is simple, satisfying, and a great way to pack in loads of veggies and protein. This version filled with asparagus, peppers, leeks, and baby broccoli is perfect for spring.

6 oz (170 g) asparagus
1 orange bell pepper
1 red bell pepper
1 yellow bell pepper
1 cup (85 g) baby broccoli
Extra virgin olive oil
2 garlic cloves, minced
1 cup (90 g) sliced leeks (about 2 medium leeks)
½ cup (120 ml) water
Sea salt and pepper, to taste
6 large eggs
3 sprigs fresh thyme
½ tsp dried oregano

Special Equipment

11-inch (28 cm) frying pan with lid

1. Wash and chop the asparagus, peppers, and broccoli into roughly ½-inch (1.25 cm) pieces of equal size for even cooking.
2. Heat about 1 tablespoon of olive oil in a large frying pan over medium heat. Add in the minced garlic and cook for 1 minute, until fragrant.
3. Add in the leeks, cooking for 5 to 6 minutes, until it begins to soften.
4. Add in the remaining vegetables, water, salt, and pepper. Cook for 10 to 12 minutes, until tender.
5. Meanwhile, whisk the eggs in a separate medium bowl. Add in salt, pepper, the thyme, and the oregano, stirring to combine.
6. Once the vegetables are cooked and the water has completely evaporated, let the vegetables cool slightly and then add them into the bowl with the whisked egg mixture. Stir well.
7. Pour everything into an 11-inch (28 cm) frying pan. Cook partially covered over medium heat for 5 to 7 minutes, until a golden crust forms on the bottom.
8. With the help of the lid, flip the frittata out and slide it back into the pan with the uncooked side down. (See Note.) Cook the other side for 4 to 5 minutes, until the frittata is firm, set, and golden brown on each side.

NOTE

Flipping a frittata is a bit of an art and sometimes a gamble. The trick? Use a large flat plate or lid and flip with confidence. Really go for it and don't hesitate. Hesitation can leave a sad frittata lying on the floor. (In Italy, they'd even say you made a "frittata," aka "a mistake.") If you'd rather play it safe, you can also finish the frittata under the broiler until it's perfectly golden and firm on top—no flipping required. If you choose this method, just be sure to use an oven-safe pan.

piatti principali

Pasta Fatta in Casa

Fresh Homemade Pasta

• • •

7 servings

There's a special magic in making pasta from scratch. It's soft and delicate in a way that dry pasta simply can't replicate. Many people think Italians make fresh pasta from scratch daily, but it's simply not true. In fact, in our house, we typically reach for high-quality dry pasta for our everyday cooking, and proudly so! Fresh pasta is something we reserve for special occasions, for when we want to slow down and make a full experience of the meal. It's perfect for a birthday, an anniversary, or a date night. This recipe celebrates the tradition and art of making fresh pasta without pressuring you to do it every weeknight.

3⅓ cups (400 g) 00 flour
4 large eggs
Semolina flour, for tossing

Special Equipment
Dough scraper (optional)
Rolling pin
Pasta machine

1. Dump the flour onto a work surface and create a well in the center using a bowl, a spoon, or your fingers.
2. Beat the eggs in a bowl and pour them into the center well.
3. Little by little, use a fork to mix a bit of flour in with the eggs until incorporated.
4. Use a dough scraper or your hands to continue gathering the dough together, making sure the eggs are blended well into the dough.
5. Knead the dough until the ingredients are fully incorporated, 5 to 10 minutes, and then shape into a ball. Wrap in plastic and rest in the fridge for 30 minutes.
6. After resting, remove the dough from the fridge. Cut off ¼ of the dough and set the rest aside, keeping it wrapped to prevent it from drying out.
7. Roll out the piece of dough, folding the ends toward the center to create a rectangle that can easily pass through a pasta machine. (See Note.)
8. Pass the dough through the widest pasta machine roller about three or four times, folding the dough onto itself each time so you strengthen the gluten. Gradually reduce the thickness of the roller until you get to the thinnest setting.
9. Cut the pasta sheets into long, thin pieces or into your preferred shapes. Repeat with the remaining dough.
10. Cook in salted, boiling water for 2 to 3 minutes (depending on thickness) and serve.

NOTE

If not using a pasta maker, on a lightly floured surface, use a rolling pin to roll out the dough as thin as possible, about 1⁄16 inches (1.5 mm). If making long pasta, loosely roll the dough into a log and use a sharp knife to cut ¼-inch (6 mm) strips. If making pasta shapes, roll out the dough in the same way, and then use the required technique or tool for your preferred shape. (There are hundreds of different shapes and each is made differently, so feel free to get creative and make your favorite!)

piatti principali

Pasta al Pesto

Pasta with Homemade Pesto

. . .

2 servings

Traditional pesto alla Genovese is made with a blend of Parmigiano Reggiano and Pecorino Romano, but in our house, we usually keep it simple with just Parmigiano Reggiano. It's still rich and fresh because it highlights the brightness of the basil, the bitterness of an excellent olive oil, and the creaminess of good cheese. Don't you dare reach for the green can when making this recipe. We're watching!

Several years ago, Alessio tried pesto in Liguria, the region where it was born, and never stopped talking about how life-changing it was. The first time he had it there, it blew his mind, and he swore he'd never been able to replicate the flavor at home or with any store-bought jar. We were recently fortunate to take a trip there together, and let me say—I get it now. Trying authenic pesto for the first time opened my eyes, and I made it a mission to try and help him recreate it outside of that beautiful Italian coastline. You just won't understand the difference until you try homemade pesto for yourself.

In spring, you can usually find fresh basil at the market, especially as the weather warms up. If it's still early in the season and your basil isn't quite fragrant yet, you can stretch it by blending in a bit of spinach or arugula for a twist. It won't be authentic pesto alla Genovese, but it will still taste amazing. Just promise us you'll use the good olive oil and the *real* Parmigiano Reggiano.

Pesto is traditionally served with trofie, a short, twisted pasta that holds the sauce well. However, we also like to toss it with gnocchi, fusilli, or spinach tortellini.

2 pinches of sea salt
½ garlic clove
20 pine nuts
4 large handfuls of small fresh basil leaves
2 tsp grated Parmigiano Reggiano
2 tsp grated Pecorino Romano (optional)
2 tbsp extra virgin olive oil
7 oz (200 g) dry trofie pasta

Special Equipment
Mortar and pestle

1. Grind the salt into a fine powder in a mortar and pestle.
2. Remove the green center from the garlic and add the half clove into the mortar, crushing and combining it with the salt.
3. Add in the pine nuts and crush them, combining them with the salt and garlic until a paste forms.
4. Begin adding the basil leaves, only three or four at a time. Use the pressure of the pestle to break up the leaves, but be careful not to create too much heat, as that will cause the basil to oxidize and turn brown.
5. Once all the basil leaves have been added, add in the Parmigiano Reggiano and continue to mix. You can also add in Pecorino Romano if desired.
6. Finally, add the olive oil to help everything blend together and become a creamy sauce.
7. Once the pesto is creamy and combined, cook the pasta according to the package instructions and drain. Stir the pesto into the freshly cooked pasta and serve.

piatti principali

Quattro Formaggi

Four Cheese Pasta

• • •

2 servings

Let's just get this out there: I've been a lifelong macaroni and cheese lover. The boxed kind, the baked kind—I love it all. Where I grew up, mac and cheese might even be considered a vegetable, so to say I'm a fan is an understatement. So, when Alessio's mom made me Quattro Formaggi on one of our first trips to Italy, I was in cheese heaven. It was creamy and rich, and it basically felt like a grown-up version of my favorite food.

This is one of the only mac and cheese–style dishes that passes Alessio's rigorous Italian approval process. Honestly? I get it. When it's made with his beloved Gorgonzola dolce, it keeps him coming back for more. Our version includes the cheeses listed below, but feel free to make it your own. Emmental, provolone, or even a bit of Brie (shh … don't tell Alessio—we're still trying to convince people he's not secretly French) can work beautifully, depending on what you have on hand. When Alessio's mom made it for me, she used a bit of local Montasio cheese, and it was otherworldly. Just make sure that the cheeses you use melt well and bring a little character to the sauce.

Whatever you do, skip the pre-shredded stuff and stay away from overly processed cheese blends. Go for cheese with personality—don't just use three different shades of cheddar and call it a day. Grate or chop your cheese fresh, stir it in gradually, and let it become a melty, luxurious sauce that Alessio would be proud of.

- 7 oz (200 g) dry penne rigate pasta
- 3½ oz (100 g) Gorgonzola dolce
- 3½ oz (100 g) Gruyère
- 3½ oz (100 g) taleggio or fontina
- ¾ cup (180 ml) whole milk
- 3½ oz (100 g) finely grated Parmigiano Reggiano, plus more for serving
- ¼ tsp ground nutmeg
- 1 tsp sea salt
- Freshly cracked pepper, to taste

1. Cook the pasta in a large pot of salted, boiling water according to the package instructions.
2. While the pasta is cooking, chop the Gorgonzola, Gruyère, and taleggio into small cubes. The smaller they are, the easier to melt later on. (P.S., don't snack on the cheese!)
3. Gradually warm the milk in a 5-quart (4.7 L) sauté pan over low heat, stirring continuously to prevent burning.
4. Once the milk is heated, add in the cubes of cheese and the Parmigiano Reggiano a little at a time (this helps prevent separation or an unwanted grainy texture), stirring so that the cheese melts and is incorporated evenly into the milk.
5. Add in the nutmeg, salt, and pepper, and stir to fully combine.
6. Once the pasta is cooked, reserve ½ cup (120 ml) of the pasta water and drain the rest. Add a splash of pasta water at a time to the cheese sauce, stirring, until smooth and creamy.
7. Stir the cooked pasta into the cheese sauce and serve with a bit of grated Parmigiano Reggiano or freshly cracked pepper.

piatti principali

Pasta Aglio, Olio, e Peperoncino

Pasta with Garlic, Oil, and Italian Chili Pepper

• • •

4 servings

This recipe is proof that a few simple ingredients can become something cherished and unforgettable. Originating from Naples, Pasta Aglio e Olio was born out of necessity. It uses typical ingredients people already had on hand—pasta, garlic, olive oil, and chili. It's a no-frills recipe, but it doesn't need them. This is Italian cooking at its best: simple, bold, flavorful.

A tip here is to use the highest-quality pasta and olive oil you can swing. There aren't a lot of ingredients to hide behind, so quality will make all the difference. Remember, with this strategy, recipes that might seem "boring" actually are "timeless."

Sea salt, to taste

11 oz (320 g) dry or 14 oz (400 g) fresh spaghetti

2 small fresh Calabrian chili peppers (can sub with 1 tsp jarred)

½ cup (120 ml) extra virgin olive oil

2 garlic cloves, thinly sliced

Chopped fresh parsley (optional)

1 Cook the spaghetti in a large pot of salted, boiling water according to the package instructions.

2 Remove the centers and the seeds from the chili peppers and slice into thin rounds.

3 Add the olive oil to a large sauté pan over very low heat. You want it as low as possible since the garlic and peppers can easily burn.

4 Add the garlic and peppers, continuing to stir and swirl the oil to prevent burning. Cook for a few minutes, until fragrant.

5 Once the pasta is cooked, ladle ⅓ to ½ cup (80 to 120 ml) pasta water into the pan with the garlic, oil, and peppers. Add in the drained pasta and toss to coat with the oil mixture.

6 Stir and cook for a couple minutes to perfect the flavors, top with parley, if desired, and then serve immediately.

piatti principali

Pasta al Limone

Lemon Pasta

• • •

4 servings

This dish is sunshine on a plate. It's made with bright citrus, rich cream, and a hint of butter—it's the perfect transition meal to bridge the coziness of winter with the freshness of spring. Citrus is technically a winter fruit, but just as the seasons start to shift, this lemon pasta reminds you that brighter days are coming.

This pasta is silky and can feel indulgent, but the lemon zest wakes everything up. Even though it combines cream, butter, and Parmigiano Reggiano, it isn't heavy. Make this as the days start getting longer and the breeze starts coming through the open windows.

- 11 oz (320 g) dry or 14 oz (400 g) fresh spaghetti
- 1 tbsp extra virgin olive oil
- 2 tbsp unsalted butter
- Juice and zest of 1 lemon, divided
- 1 cup (240 ml) heavy cream
- ¼ cup (15 g) finely chopped fresh parsley
- Sea salt and pepper, to taste
- Grated Parmigiano Reggiano, for garnish

1. Cook the pasta in a large pot of salted, boiling water according to the package instructions.
2. Warm the olive oil and melt the butter in a large sauté pan over medium-low heat.
3. Once the butter has melted, reduce the heat to low and add in the lemon juice and half of the zest, stirring and cooking for 1 minute.
4. Ladle ⅓ to ½ cup (80 to 120 ml) pasta water into the pan, drain the rest of the pasta water, and add the pasta to the pan. Stir to combine.
5. Add in the cream, stirring and cooking for a couple minutes to fully combine.
6. Remove the pan from the heat and add in the remaining lemon zest and the parsley, salt, and pepper. Stir to combine.
7. Serve with a bit of grated Parmigiano Reggiano over the top.

piatti principali

Pasta Carbonara

• • •

2 servings

When Alessio and I took our first trip to Rome, we made it our mission to eat the best pasta carbonara the city had to offer. After a long day wandering through the Vatican and walking for miles trying to hit all the historic Roman sites, we stumbled (by total accident) upon a little place called Ristorante da Michele on Via Merulana. It wasn't on any list or guide—we just got lucky. First bite of the carbonara? Life. Changing. I still remember how we both took a bite, looked up, and locked eyes at the same time. We had a moment of understanding that we were eating something truly magical and without a word, we both looked back down at our plates and kept shoveling in the goodness. Creamy, salty, and rich, it was easily one of the best things we'd ever eaten. We've tried so many others since, but nothing's quite matched the magic of that first plate. So, of course, we had to try and recreate it at home.

A lot of people outside of Italy think carbonara includes cream, garlic, onions, or other extras. True Roman carbonara is simple: egg yolks, Pecorino Romano, guanciale, black pepper, and pasta. No cream because when it's done right, it doesn't need anything else to make it silky smooth.

And don't worry about the eggs being "raw." The heat from the just-cooked pasta is enough to gently cook them into a safe, rich, velvety sauce. No scrambling, no weird textures. This version is our love letter to that unforgettable evening in Rome that forever changed us and reminded us of the magic of Italy.

- 7 oz (200 g) dry spaghetti
- ½ cup (80 g) diced guanciale
- 3 large egg yolks
- 2 oz (57 g) finely grated Pecorino Romano, plus more for garnish
- Freshly cracked black pepper, to taste, plus more for serving

1. Cook the spaghetti in a large pot of salted, boiling water according to the package instructions.
2. Meanwhile, cook the guanciale in a large saucepan over medium heat for 4 to 5 minutes. (You don't need olive oil here because the guanciale will release fat to prevent sticking.) Once cooked, the guanciale should be crispy and golden brown. Turn off the heat.
3. Whisk the egg yolks in a small bowl and add in the Pecorino Romano and black pepper, to taste.
4. Take a spoonful of guanciale and rendered fat from the pan and stir it into the egg mixture to temper the eggs.
5. Once the pasta is cooked, reserve ⅓ to ½ cup (80 to 120 ml) of the pasta water and drain the rest. Quickly add the pasta to the pan with the guanciale.
6. Immediately add the egg mixture and reserved pasta water to the pasta and stir vigorously for 1 to 2 minutes until a thick, creamy sauce forms. The heat from the pasta will slightly cook the egg and make the sauce into a cream.
7. Top with more grated Pecorino Romano and freshly cracked pepper.

piatti principali

Lasagne ai Carciofi

Pesto Artichoke Lasagna

• • •

6 servings

This might be one of my favorite recipes in the entire book. I first had a version of this dish during a trip to Lake Como, and after just one bite, I knew I had to try and recreate it in our kitchen. It's creamy and full of flavor. Even with its richness, it's still perfect for spring since it incorporates basil and artichokes.

It's not your typical lasagna, and that's what makes it so special. It's a dish with a wow factor. Instead of traditional meat sauce, this one is layered with fresh pesto, delicate artichoke hearts, and creamy besciamella. It's an unexpected way to reimagine lasagna for spring. Trust us, everyone at the table will be asking for seconds.

This recipe calls for both Homemade Pesto (page 56) and Besciamella (Béchamel Sauce, page 224), so feel free to make those ahead of time if you're planning this for a dinner party or special occasion. It's 100% worth it.

1¼ cups (315 g) Homemade Pesto (page 56), or store-bought pesto
4 to 5 cups (1 to 1.2 L) Besciamella (Béchamel Sauce, page 224)
7 fresh artichokes
Juice of 1 lemon
1 to 2 tbsp extra virgin olive oil
1 garlic clove, minced
1 tsp sea salt
Pepper, to taste
Splash of vegetable broth or water
14 oz (400 g) dry oven-ready lasagna noodles
4¼ oz (120 g) freshly grated Parmigiano Reggiano
3½ oz (100 g) grated provolone

Special Equipment

9 × 13-inch (23 × 33 cm) baking dish

NOTE

Use a sharp knife to cut off the top half of the leaves and most of the stem. Carefully use your hands to peel off the tough outer leaves, being wary of the thorns. With a paring knife, cut/shave off the remaining hard, darker green peel until you get to the soft inner portion that is lighter in color. Cut the heart in half and scoop out the choke with a spoon or paring knife. Only the heart and the soft inner leaves should remain.

1. Prepare the pesto and besciamella sauces if making from scratch.
2. Preheat the oven to 350°F (180°C). Grease a 9 × 13-inch (23 × 33 cm) baking dish.
3. Prepare the artichokes by removing the stems, tough outer leaves, chokes, and thorny tips, leaving only the hearts and tender inner leaves. (See Note.) Cut the artichokes into quarters and then slice into thin pieces and place them in a large bowl of cold water and lemon juice.
4. Heat the olive oil in a large sauté pan. Add in the garlic and cook for 1 minute, until fragrant.
5. Add in the artichoke hearts, salt, and pepper, and cook for 7 to 8 minutes. If needed, you can add a splash of broth or water to help them cook. Once the artichokes are soft, remove them from the heat and set aside.
6. Spread ¼ cup (65 g) of the pesto and ¼ cup (60 ml) of the besciamella on the bottom of the baking dish. This helps to prevent sticking.
7. Add a layer of the lasagna noodles and top with some of the pesto, besciamella, artichokes, Parmigiano Reggiano, and provolone. Be sure to reserve enough of each to complete the layers in the next step.
8. Continue with a second layer, using the same order as before. Continue adding layers until everything is finished (at least three layers in total), but make sure to reserve a generous amount of artichoke, pesto, and besciamella for the top. Sprinkle with a generous amount of Parmigiano Reggiano.
9. Bake for 40 to 45 minutes. If needed, broil on high for a few minutes at the end to make the cheese crust golden brown and bubbly.
10. Remove from the oven and allow the lasagna to rest for 10 to 15 minutes before slicing.

piatti principali

Polpette di Spinaci e Ricotta

Spinach and Ricotta "Meatballs"

. . .

4 servings

Alessio made these on a whim one day, messing around in the kitchen, and they've been a staple for us ever since. It might come as a surprise, but we actually don't eat a lot of meat, so we're always looking for meals that are hearty and satisfying on their own. These "meatballs" are soft and cheesy on the inside and crispy on the outside with a delicate covering of breadcrumbs.

If you're one of those people (like me) who buys spinach with the best of intentions—salads, smoothies, etc., only to watch it wilt sadly in the back of the fridge, then this recipe has come to save you. Pull out that spinach, cook it down, roll it up into some cute little balls, and bake it into something you'll truly enjoy and look forward to enjoy eating.

We love serving these with a side of Verdure al Forno (Oven-Roasted Vegetables, page 100) or tucked into a sandwich. You can also plate them on top of a bit of simple tomato sauce (like the Spaghetti al Pomodoro on page 108) for the more "classic" meatball vibe.

- 1 tbsp extra virgin olive oil
- 1 lb (454 g) fresh spinach
- 8 oz (227 g) ricotta, strained if required
- 2 oz (57 g) freshly finely grated Parmigiano Reggiano
- ⅓ cup (40 g) dry breadcrumbs, plus more for rolling
- Sea salt and pepper, to taste
- 1 large egg

1. Preheat the oven to 400°F (200°C). Line a baking sheet with parchment paper.
2. Heat the olive oil in a large saucepan over medium-low heat and cook the spinach until wilted, about 3 minutes. Let cool and then squeeze out as much water as possible from the spinach. Chop into fine pieces.
3. Combine the ricotta, Parmigiano Reggiano, breadcrumbs, salt, and pepper in a large bowl.
4. Stir in the spinach and mix until fully combined. Place more breadcrumbs in a small bowl. Whisk the egg in a separate small bowl.
5. Roll the spinach mixture into golf ball–sized "meatballs" and place them on the prepared baking sheet. Dip each ball into the egg and then roll in the breadcrumbs. Make sure each is fully coated and then place it back on the prepared baking sheet.
6. Bake for 20 to 25 minutes, until golden and crispy. Broil on high for 2 to 3 minutes, if needed, to achieve a more golden crust. Be careful not to burn.

piatti principali

Pollo al Limone

Lemon Chicken

. . .

4 servings

This isn't your typical grilled chicken breast with lemon juice drizzled on top. It's something simpler, brighter, and honestly, more delicious. Lightly dredged in lemon juice and flour and then browned and simmered in an easy lemon-thyme sauce, this chicken dish is full of flavor but still quick to pull off. Make it on a night when you're craving something fresh and zesty. It's best served with Verdure al Forno (Oven-Roasted Vegetables, page 100) or Patate in Padella (Pan-Fried Potatoes, page 39).

- 4 thinly sliced chicken cutlets (scallopini), about 1 lb/454 g
- Juice of 1½ lemons, divided
- ½ cup (60 g) all-purpose flour, plus 1 tbsp for sauce
- 1 tbsp extra virgin olive oil
- 3 sprigs fresh thyme
- Sea salt and freshly cracked black pepper, to taste
- Zest of 1 lemon
- ¾ cup (180 ml) water

1. Pound the chicken cutlets flat for even cooking.
2. Place the juice of one lemon in a shallow bowl and spread the flour onto a plate. Add a chicken cutlet to the bowl, turning to coat well in the juice. Transfer the chicken to the plate and coat it in the flour, shaking off any excess. Repeat with the remaining chicken.
3. Heat the olive oil in a large frying pan over medium-high heat. Add the thyme sprigs and the chicken. Cook the chicken for 2 to 3 minutes on each side to develop a golden crust.
4. Salt and pepper the chicken and then remove from the pan and set aside.
5. Add the juice of the half lemon and the lemon zest to the same pan.
6. Add the extra tablespoon of flour and the water, whisking until smooth.
7. Return the chicken to the pan and cook, turning occasionally, until the mixture is hot and the chicken is cooked through, about 2 to 5 minutes per side.
8. To serve, remove the thyme, arrange the chicken on a platter or serving plates, and drizzle with the sauce. Finish with freshly cracked pepper.

Torta di Carote

Italian Carrot Cake

• • •

10 servings

This is not the carrot cake you're probably thinking of. There's no cinnamon, nutmeg, walnuts, or cream cheese frosting here—and no towering layers either. Italian carrot cake is a completely different kind of dessert. It's light and tender, it's subtly sweet, and it has a beautiful pale orange color that wows on the table.

The first time Alessio told me we were going to make carrot cake, I was picturing the spiced version I grew up with in the South—dense, rich, and covered in creamy frosting. So when he pulled out this recipe, I was understandably confused. But we made it anyway, and I was so pleasantly surprised by how soft and simple it was. Now it's the only carrot cake we make!

We always dust the top with a little powdered sugar and serve it as an afternoon snack, dessert, or yes, even breakfast. It's a lovely reminder that, sometimes, unexpected versions end up being the ones you love most.

Unsalted butter, for greasing
2¼ cups (270 g) cake flour
2 tsp baking powder
¼ to ½ tsp sea salt
3 medium carrots (9 oz/255 g), peeled and chopped
⅓ cup (80 ml) orange juice
3 large eggs
¾ cup (150 g) granulated sugar
¾ cup (150 g) granulated sugar
⅓ cup (80 ml) avocado oil
1 tsp almond extract
1 tsp vanilla extract
Powdered sugar, for dusting

Special Equipment

8- or 9-inch (20 or 23 cm) round cake pan
Food processor
Electric mixer
Wooden spoon

1. Preheat the oven to 350°F (180°C). Grease an 8- or 9-inch (20 or 23 cm) round cake pan with butter and line the bottom with parchment paper.
2. Whisk together the flour, baking powder, and salt in a medium bowl.
3. Blend the carrots and orange juice in a food processor, until finely chopped (you want it somewhere between grated carrots and a puree).
4. Beat together the eggs, sugar, and orange zest in a large bowl with an electric mixer for 2 minutes, until creamy, frothy, and pale yellow.
5. Add the carrot mixture, avocado oil, and almond and vanilla extracts, and use a wooden spoon to mix well and combine.
6. Add the flour mixture, a little at a time as you mix, being careful not to overmix.
7. Scrape the batter into the pan and bake for 35 to 40 minutes, until a toothpick inserted into the cake comes out clean.
8. Let the cake cool for 10 minutes before turning out onto a wire rack to cool completely. Dust with powdered sugar just before serving.

Torta alla Ricotta e Cioccolato

Chocolate Chip Ricotta Cake

• • •

10 servings

On one of my first trips to Italy, I remember walking into the breakfast room of a hotel and doing a double take. Instead of the eggs, sausage, and toast that I was used to, the table was piled high with cakes, pastries, and croissants (many of them dusted with powdered sugar and filled with jam, cream, or Nutella). It felt more like a dessert buffet than a breakfast. To be completely honest, I wasn't mad about it.

One thing that caught my eye was a soft ricotta cake speckled with dark chocolate chips. It was light, barely sweet at all, and very satisfying alongside my cappuccino. I couldn't believe I was in Italy, eating cake for breakfast, and it wasn't only accepted—it was expected.

This version is inspired by that very first Italian hotel breakfast. It's easy to make, not too sweet, and just rich enough. And yes, we're totally expecting you to eat a slice in the morning.

Unsalted butter, for greasing
35 oz (1 kg) ricotta, strained if needed
3 large eggs
1 cup (200 g) granulated sugar
¾ cup (90 g) all-purpose flour
1 tsp vanilla bean paste
¾ cup (170 g) dark chocolate chips, divided
Powdered sugar, for dusting (optional)

Special Equipment

9-inch (23 cm) springform pan

1. Preheat the oven to 350°F (180°C). Grease a 9-inch (23 cm) springform pan with the butter.
2. Combine the ricotta, eggs, and sugar in a large bowl.
3. Stir in the flour and vanilla bean paste.
4. Fold in ½ cup (113 g) of the chocolate chips.
5. Pour the batter into the greased cake pan. Sprinkle the remaining ¼ cup (57 g) chocolate chips on top of the batter and bake for 1 hour, or until set and golden brown on top.
6. Once baked, turn off the oven and allow the torta to cool inside with the door ajar for 1 hour.
7. Cover the torta and refrigerate for 4 hours or overnight, until cold.
8. Dust with powdered sugar, if desired.

Crostata ai Frutti di Bosco

Berry Tart

• • •

6 servings

This tart is the kind of dessert you'll spot behind glass in a typical Italian pasticceria. It's glossy, colorful, and almost too pretty to eat. It's a go-to in Italy for a good reason. Whenever we're visiting Alessio's family or friends, we love stopping by the bakery to pick one up, either as a sweet offering for a dinner party or as a breakfast treat alongside a tray of pasticcini. While it might not be as globally famous as tiramisù or cannoli, Crostata di Frutta is a true Italian favorite, especially in the spring when strawberries, raspberries, and blueberries start popping up at the farmer's market.

For the crust:

6 tablespoons unsalted butter, very cold, plus more for greasing
1 cup (120 g) all-purpose flour, sifted, plus more for dusting
½ cup (60 g) powdered sugar, sifted
Zest of ½ lemon
1 large egg yolk

For the cream custard:

1 cup (240 ml) whole milk
¼ cup (60 ml) heavy cream
1 tsp vanilla bean paste
3 large egg yolks
⅓ cup (66 g) granulated sugar
2 tbsp cornstarch

For the topping:

1 cup (145 g) strawberries
1 cup (125 g) raspberries
1 cup (140 g) blackberries
1 cup (150 g) blueberries

Special Equipment

Food processor
14-inch (36 cm) rectangular tart pan
Rolling pin
Pie weights or beans

1. *To make the crust:* Cut the butter into cubes. Add the cubed butter and the flour to a food processor and blend until a sandy, crumbly mixture is formed.
2. Add the butter mixture, powdered sugar, and lemon zest to a large bowl.
3. Add in the egg yolk and lightly knead the dough until it forms a ball. Don't overdo this because you don't want the heat of your hands to warm up the butter and pastry.
4. Flatten the dough into a small disk and wrap it in plastic wrap. Set in the fridge to chill for 30 minutes to 1 hour.
5. *To make the cream custard:* Warm the milk and heavy cream in a large saucepan over low heat. Add in the vanilla bean paste.
6. Once the mixture is frothy and almost boiling, turn off the heat and allow to sit for about 5 minutes.
7. Meanwhile, whisk together the egg yolks and sugar in a large bowl to make a smooth cream.
8. Add in the cornstarch, stirring to combine.
9. Add a small amount of the milk mixture to the egg mixture, stirring to temper the egg mixture. Combine the mixtures and whisk thoroughly.
10. Heat on low and stir continuously while thickening the combined mixture, 5 to 7 minutes.
11. Once thick, pour the custard into a large dish or bowl, cover with plastic wrap, and allow to cool to room temperature. Then place the custard in the fridge for 1 hour.
12. While the custard is chilling, preheat the oven to 350°F (180°C). Butter and flour a 14-inch (36 cm) rectangular tart pan.
13. Remove the pastry dough from the fridge and place it on a lightly floured surface.
14. Use a rolling pin to roll out the dough to the length and width of your tart pan, making sure it's about ¼- to ½ inch (6 mm to 1.25 cm) thick.

15 Press the dough into the tart pan and use a fork to prick the base and around the edges.

16 Blind bake the crust by filling it with parchment paper and pie weights (or dry beans). Bake for 20 minutes, or until golden.

17 Remove from the oven, remove the paper and weights, and allow the crust to cool.

18 Once fully cooled, spoon the chilled custard cream into the crust.

19 *To make the topping:* Clean the fruit and either leave it whole or slice it. Place it on top of the tart to fully cover the custard. Serve!

Panna Cotta ai Lamponi

Raspberry Panna Cotta

. . .

6 servings

Panna cotta is one of the most classic Italian desserts. It's elegant, subtle, and extremely versatile. It originates from the Piedmont region of Northern Italy and is often served at restaurants or family gatherings when you want something that feels special but not extravagant.

This version adds raspberries for a touch of brightness and a pop of color. The cream is infused with vanilla, poured over the berries, and chilled until it's lusciously smooth. It feels fancy with very little effort. The kind of thing that will impress your guests. It's a dessert you'll find everywhere, from the humble trattorias to the refined, Michelin-star restaurants across Italy. A perfect example of "less is more" with Italian cooking.

4 gelatin sheets, gold 200 bloom
1 cup (125 g) fresh raspberries, plus more for garnish
2 cups (480 ml) heavy cream
⅔ cup (80 g) powdered sugar
1 vanilla bean pod
Mint leaves, for garnish

Special Equipment

Fine-mesh sieve
Six 6-oz (170 g) ramekins or serving glasses

1 Soak the gelatin sheets in cold water for about 10 minutes.
2 Meanwhile, wash the raspberries and dry them well.
3 In a medium pan over low heat, begin warming the cream and sugar together, stirring to dissolve the sugar, 2 to 3 minutes.
4 Slice open the vanilla pod and scrape out the seeds. Add the pod and seeds to the cream and sugar mixture.
5 Continue to warm the cream and sugar mixture until it's just about to boil, but do not let it boil. Whisk constantly to prevent burning.
6 Quickly squeeze out the gelatin and place it in a large bowl.
7 Once the cream and sugar mixture is almost at the boiling point, strain it through a fine-mesh sieve over the gelatin in the bowl. Discard any solids that remain.
8 Stir to dissolve the gelatin.
9 Place a few raspberries into the bottom of each ramekin.
10 Pour enough cream to fill each ramekin halfway, fully covering the first layer of raspberries. Place into the fridge for about 1 hour to chill.
11 Cover the remaining cream loosely with plastic to keep it from drying out. Set aside on the counter.
12 After 1 hour, remove the molds from the fridge and place a few more raspberries in each. Cover with a second layer of cream.
13 Place in the fridge for another 2 hours, or until completely firm.
14 To help remove the panna cotta from the ramekins, dip them in hot water for a few seconds. Use a sharp knife to slice around the edge and flip the panna cotta out onto a serving dish.
15 Decorate with additional raspberries and mint leaves.

NOTE

As an alternative to using the ramekins, you can make the panna cotta in small serving glasses and skip step 14.

Torta Mimosa

Mimosa Sponge Cake

• • •

10 servings

Torta Mimosa is a beautiful Italian cake traditionally served on March 8th to celebrate International Women's Day, or La Festa della Donna. Its name comes from the bright yellow mimosa flower that is traditionally given as a gift to women on that day. The cake is decorated with cubes of sponge cake to mimic the delicate blossoms of the mimosa tree. It's light, elegant, and a unique dessert to serve up to family or guests.

The first time I had this cake was on Alessio's mom's birthday, which just happens to fall on International Women's Day. We picked up the cake to celebrate both occasions, and I was immediately drawn in by its charming appearance. It looked just like a little bouquet. The first bite was even better … soft and creamy, with a hint of citrus.

Most people in the US have never heard of this dessert. It's fun to assemble, beautiful to look at, and a guaranteed conversation starter. The best part about it, though? It's the perfect way to celebrate the strong women in your life and bring a little sunshine to their table.

Unsalted butter, for greasing
Powdered sugar, for dusting

For the sponge cake:

8 large eggs, room temperature
1 tsp vanilla bean paste
⅛ tsp sea salt
1¼ cups (250 g) granulated sugar
1¼ cups (160 g) all-purpose flour
¾ cup (130 g) potato starch
Zest of 1 lemon

For the diplomat cream:

2 cups (480 ml) whole milk
1 cup (240 ml) heavy cream, divided
1 tsp vanilla bean paste
5 large egg yolks
¾ cup (150 g) granulated sugar
3 tbsp cornstarch
2½ tbsp powdered sugar

For the syrup:

½ cup (120 ml) water
⅓ cup (66 g) granulated sugar
2 tbsp orange liqueur, such as Grand Marnier (you can use lemon juice for a nonalcoholic version)

Special Equipment

Two 8-inch (20 cm) round cake pans
Electric mixer with a whisk attachment
Cake stand or serving platter

• • •

1. Preheat the oven to 325°F (165°C). Grease two 8-inch (20 cm) round cake pans with butter and line the bottoms with parchment paper.
2. *To make the sponge cake:* Add the eggs to a large bowl and use an electric mixer with a whisk attachment to whisk until blended and frothy.
3. Add in the vanilla bean paste, salt, and lemon zest, and mix to combine.
4. Little by little, add in the sugar and continue to whisk for about 15 minutes, or until the mixture has doubled in volume and is light and creamy.
5. Sift the flour and potato starch into the egg mixture. Fold them in gently, taking care not to deflate the mixture.
6. Equally divide the cake batter between the prepared cake pans.
7. Bake on the middle rack for 50 to 55 minutes, until a toothpick inserted in the center comes out clean.
8. Let rest in the pans for 15 minutes before removing. Then place on a cooling rack to cool completely.

9 *To make the diplomat cream:* While the cakes are baking, combine the milk, ½ cup (120 ml) heavy cream, and vanilla bean paste in a small saucepan over low heat and heat until almost boiling. Stir occasionally to prevent burning.

10 While that is warming, whisk together the egg yolks and sugar in a medium bowl, until smooth and creamy.

11 Sift in the cornstarch and stir to combine.

12 Pour ½ cup (120 ml) of the milk mixture into the egg mixture, stirring to temper the egg mixture. Add the egg mixture to the milk mixture and stir constantly over low heat, for 5 to 10 minutes until thickened. Scrape into a wide, shallow dish. Cover with plastic wrap and set aside to cool completely.

13 Using an electric mixer, whisk together the remaining heavy cream and the powdered sugar in a small bowl until soft peaks form. Fold into the cooled cream until combined.

14 Cover and place in the fridge for 30 to 60 minutes to fully set.

15 *To make the syrup:* In the meantime, add the water, sugar, and orange liqueur to a small saucepan over medium heat. Stir continuously until the sugar is dissolved. Pour into a small bowl and let cool.

16 *To assemble the cake:* Once everything is fully cooled, use a serrated knife to remove the brown outer crust from the tops and sides of each cake.

17 Slice one cake horizontally into three equal layers.

18 Cut the other cake into even, ½-inch (1.25 cm) cubes. Set these aside.

19 Place a small dollop of the cream mixture onto a cake stand or serving platter to secure the cake and then place the first layer of cake on top. Using a spoon, drizzle one-third of the syrup over the cake. Then spread one-quarter of the cream mixture evenly over the top, taking care to make sure it is level.

20 Add the second layer and repeat the process with the syrup and cream.

21 Add the third and final layer, using the remaining cream to coat the top and sides of the cake.

22 Gently press the cake cubes into the top and sides of the cake, ensuring the entire surface is covered.

23 Once the cake is fully covered, chill in the fridge for at least 2 hours to firm up. Dust with extra powdered sugar just before serving.

bevande

Succo ACE

ACE Juice

. . .

4 servings

The first time I saw ACE juice, I was standing in a hotel breakfast room, staring at a glowing orange pitcher next to the orange juice. Everyone was pouring it into their glasses, and I thought, "*What* is that?" Alessio explained that it was ACE, an Italian favorite made with oranges, carrots, and lemons and named for the vitamins it's rich in—A, C, and E.

It's sweet, tangy, and extremely refreshing, almost like a little glass of sunshine. Now, whenever we're in Italy, I seek it out. Whether we're dining at another hotel breakfast, snacking on a croissant and cappuccino at a cafe, or grabbing a carton to take home to Alessio's mom's house, ACE is always a part of my breakfast order.

Alessio loves it, too, and it's become a little morning ritual we can share together. If you've never had it before, this is your chance to bring the taste of a bright Italian morning into your own kitchen.

8 carrots
4 oranges
2 lemons
1½ cups (360 ml) water

Special Equipment
Electric juicer

1 Clean and peel the carrots, oranges, and lemons.
2 Chop everything into 2-to-3-inch (5 to 7.5 cm) pieces.
3 Slowly add the pieces to an electric juicer, adding a bit of the water in between as you continue to juice.
4 Mix the juice well and serve very cold.

The Art of an Italian Sunday Lunch

In Italy, Sunday lunch isn't just a meal, it's a full event. Whether you're feeding four or fourteen, it's about gathering with people you love and staying at the table long after the food is gone. This section is your blueprint for hosting your own springtime pranzo della domenica. Celebrate the warmer days with a cozy, laughter-filled afternoon—it's an Italian weekend ritual you'll never want to skip.

. . .

The Vibe

Time: Prepare to start eating around 1:00pm and expect to linger a few hours into the late afternoon.

Setting: A sunlit table, indoors or al fresco—doesn't matter! Fresh flowers, ceramic platters piled with food, and lots of gathered mismatched, charming details.

Energy: No rushing allowed. Now is the perfect time to teach your friends and family about il dolce far niente (the sweetness of doing nothing). A little jazz or classic Italian music. Glasses never empty. Guests helping with the dishes. Kids running around. Lots of stories and laughter.

. . .

The Traditional Flow

1. **Aperitivo:** light spritzes or Prosecco and a small bite (olives, taralli, chips, or crostini)
2. **Antipasto:** cured meats, cheeses, pickled veggies
3. **Primo:** a pasta or risotto dish that sets the tone of the second course
4. **Secondo & Contorno:** roasted meat or fish with sides like sautéed greens or potatoes
5. **Dolce:** a simple cake, a fruit tart, or fresh fruit
6. **Caffè & Digestivo:** espresso and maybe a grappa, limoncello, or amaro to close things out

. . .

The Menus

COZY AND CLASSIC

Antipasto: Insalata di Fave (page 35)

Primo: Risotto agli Asparagi (page 48)

Secondo: Pollo al Limone (page 71) with Patate in Padella (page 39)

Contorno: Asparagi al Forno (page 36)

Dolce: Crostata ai Frutti di Bosco (page 76)

Caffè & Digestivo: Prosecco, sparkling water, still water, Spritz Aperol (page 135)

ELEGANT VEGETARIAN

Antipasto: Sformato di Carciofi (page 43) and spring Bruschetta (page 40)

Primo: Pasta al Pesto (page 56)

Contorno: Polpette di Spinaci e Ricotta (page 68) with a light tomato sauce (page 108)

Dolce: Panna Cotta ai Lamponi (page 79)

Bevande: Fresh mint and lemon sparkling water, Prosecco

Set the Scene

- Prep as much as you can the day before so you can enjoy the meal, too, and don't feel pressure to make everything from scratch. Treat your guests to a few special showstoppers.
- Add a table runner or a few taper candles, even in daylight—a little decor goes a long way. You can also use clusters of fresh vegetables of the season as centerpieces.
- Set the table before guests arrive. It doesn't need to be perfect, but it should say, "We're expecting you." It makes your guests excited from the moment they step in the door.

. . .

Welcome Your Guests

- Always offer a drink when your guests arrive—immediately. Water, wine, something bubbly. It doesn't matter what. The second someone walks in, you offer them a beverage.
- Have a snack on the table—even if you're still cooking. A small bowl of olives, breadsticks, and a little cheese. Something that says, "Welcome, and please nibble while I stir this risotto."

. . .

Savor the Meal

- Enjoy what's in season: peas, artichokes, fava beans, spring herbs (think bright, fresh, and lots of green).
- Make enough for seconds. There is no such thing as "just enough" in Italian hosting. Leftovers are a love language. Lean into that stereotype of always offering more food and saying, "Mangia!"
- Serve family style: platters in the middle; everyone helps themselves and helps to pass the plates around.
- Don't clear plates too fast—Italians linger at the table. Let the conversation stretch. Remember to take your time. A proper Sunday lunch can stretch for hours. Let it. Sit back. Pour another glass. The dirty dishes can wait.

Estate

Summer

antipasti e contorni

Polpo e Patate

Octopus and Potatoes

. . .

4 servings

If you've been following us for a while, you already know that Alessio is the seafood lover in our house. Octopus? One of his favorites. Me? Let's just say I've been on a journey to discover a new love for seafood, and Italian recipes like this one with octopus and potatoes help to win me over. Polpo e Patate is a summer staple, especially in Southern Italy and along the coast. The octopus becomes melt-in-your-mouth soft and then it's paired with olive oil–glossed potatoes and the fresh taste of lemon.

We've kept this version simple, just like what you'd find at a family lunch. Once you get the technique down, feel free to experiment with different add-ins like celery, capers, onions, or even olives. However you serve it, it's the kind of dish that can win over seafood skeptics just like me and make us say, "Okay, maybe just one more bite."

2 lbs (907 g) octopus
3 bay leaves
2 lbs (907 g) yellow potatoes
¼ cup (15 g) finely chopped fresh parsley
Lemon zest

For the dressing:

⅔ cup (160 ml) extra virgin olive oil
Juice of ½ lemon
Sea salt and pepper, to taste

1. Clean the octopus, remove the beak, and rinse under cold water.
2. Bring a large pot of salted water to a boil. Add the bay leaves.
3. Once boiling, dip the tentacles of the octopus into the water three or four times to curl. Then place the octopus fully into the water.
4. Cook covered for 40 minutes, skimming any foam that collects on the surface. When the octopus is finished cooking, remove the pot from the heat and let the octopus cool completely in the pot of water.
5. While the octopus is cooking and cooling, set a second large pot of salted water over high heat. (See Note.) Scrub the potatoes, peel them, and rinse them in water. Chop the potatoes into 1-inch (2.5 cm) cubes and place them in the water once boiling. Cook for about 15 to 18 minutes until fork tender. Drain and set aside to cool completely.
6. Once the octopus is cooled completely, drain it well and cut it into 1-inch (2.5 cm) pieces.
7. *To make the dressing:* In a small bowl, whisk together the olive oil, lemon juice, and salt and pepper.
8. In a large bowl, mix the potato and octopus.
9. Just before serving, pour in the dressing and the parsley and toss gently to combine. Garnish with fresh lemon zest and serve immediately.

TIP

This is the traditional method of cooking Polpo e Patate. However, to elevate the flavors even more, you can cook the potatoes in the water from the octopus.

antipasti e contorni

Arancine

• • •

6 to 8 servings

There are few things Sicilians take more seriously than arancine—except, perhaps, what to call them. In Palermo, it's "arancina" (feminine), named for its round, orange-like shape. In Catania, it's "arancino" (masculine), and you often see it shaped into a cone, based on the iconic silhouette of Mount Etna. In Sicily, you're expected to pick a side. You'll notice here that we chose the feminine, but please don't hold it against us, Catania! We decided that for beginner cooks, forming the balls into a rounded shape would be easier than trying to nail the cone. It's as simple as that.

Regardless of the name or gender, these golden-fried rice balls are the stuff of street food dreams. They are delicious and hearty and, in our version, stuffed with a traditional ragù filling. Once you master the classic base, the variations are endless. Try spinach and cheese (we had one in Erice that changed our lives) or mushroom and Besciamella (Béchamel Sauce, page 224). Whatever way you shape them or stuff them, one thing's for sure: It's impossible to eat just one.

For the risotto:

4½ cups (1.1 L) water or vegetable broth
1 tsp sea salt
½ tsp saffron threads
4 tbsp unsalted butter
1 small yellow onion, finely diced
2 cups (400 g) dry arborio rice
3½ oz (100 g) grated Parmigiano Reggiano

For the filling:

2 tbsp unsalted butter
1 tbsp extra virgin olive oil
½ small yellow onion, chopped
4 oz (113 g) ground beef
⅔ cup (100 g) peas
½ cup (120 ml) water
2 tbsp tomato paste
Sea salt and pepper, to taste
2½ oz (71 g) fresh mozzarella, cubed

For frying:

2 large eggs
1 cup (120 g) all-purpose flour
1½ cups (180 g) dry breadcrumbs
6 cups (1.4 L) frying oil

Special Equipment

Candy or deep-fry thermometer

1 *To make the risotto:* Warm the water or broth in a 2-quart (2 L) saucepan over medium heat with the salt and saffron.

2 Melt the butter in a large sauté pan over medium-low heat. Add the diced onion, stir, and cook for 5 to 7 minutes, until golden. Be careful not to burn the onion.

3 Add the rice to the pan and toast for 3 minutes.

4 Ladle ⅔ to 1 cup (160 to 240 ml) of the broth into the rice, stir, and cook until almost evaporated. Before it's dry, ladle in another ⅓ to ½ cup (80 to 120 ml) of liquid, continuing to stir and add more liquid as it's absorbed. Repeat until the rice is cooked, about 15 minutes. Remove from the heat and add the Parmigiano Reggiano. Stir until creamy.

5 Set aside and allow to cool completely.

6 *To make the filling:* While the risotto is cooling, melt together the butter and olive oil in a large sauté pan over medium-low heat.

7 Add the onion and cook until soft and golden, 5 to 7 minutes.

8 Add in the ground beef and stir, breaking up the meat. Cook until browned, 8 to 10 minutes.

9 Add the peas, water, and tomato paste, stirring to combine. Cook for 10 to 15 minutes.

10 Season with salt and pepper and set aside to cool.

11 *To form the arancine:* Have a baking sheet or large plate available. Divide the cooled risotto into eight equal balls. Each should be about the size of a small orange (about 2.5 inches/6.25 cm across).

12 Holding a ball in your hand, make a hole in the center and stuff it with 1 tablespoon of the beef mixture and a cube of mozzarella. Use your hands to enclose the filling, shaping it into a ball. Set it on the prepared baking sheet and repeat for the remaining arancine.

13 *To fry the arancine:* Line a tray or wire rack with paper towels. Whisk the eggs in a shallow dish. Place the flour and breadcrumbs on two separate plates.

14 Pour the frying oil into a deep pot and heat over medium-high heat.

15 While the oil is heating up, roll each arancine ball in the flour, shake to remove any excess flour, dip in the egg, and then roll in the breadcrumbs.

16 When the oil is 350°F (180°C), add a couple of arancine to the pot, making sure not to crowd them in the oil.

17 Rotate and fry them until deep, golden brown, 7 to 8 minutes.

18 Transfer the cooked arancine to the prepared tray. If desired, you can keep them warm in the oven while you fry in batches; however, you can also warm them up after all are finished.

Fiori di Zucca

Stuffed Zucchini Flowers

...

4 to 6 servings

There's something almost magical about eating fried zucchini flowers. It's like discovering a hidden gem in the garden and almost wondering, "Am I really allowed to eat this?" If you've never tried them, the idea might sound surprising: eating the flowers from a vegetable plant. However, in Italy, they're a delicacy.

The flowers are delicate and fleeting, usually picked in the early morning when they're wide and open and easiest to stuff. Finding them on a restaurant menu feels like you've won the lottery.

Traditionally, they're filled with creamy cheeses and anchovies and then fried in a light batter until crispy and golden. In Roman cuisine, you'll often find them stuffed and fried at trattorias during the summer months. But once you try them at home, you'll understand why Italians rush to buy them from the markets before they disappear for the season. They are truly a celebration of summer.

For the flowers and filling:

6 anchovies in oil, drained
4 oz (113 g) ricotta, strained if needed
2 oz (57 g) fresh mozzarella, shredded
1 oz (28 g) grated Pecorino Romano
1 large egg, lightly whisked
Sea salt and pepper, to taste
12 zucchini flowers (See Tip.)

For frying:

4 to 5 cups (1 to 1.2 L) frying oil

For the batter:

1 cup (120 g) all-purpose flour
Pinch of sea salt
1 tsp granulated sugar
1½ cups (360 ml) sparkling water, very cold

Special Equipment

Candy or deep-fry thermometer

1. *To prepare the flowers and filling:* Slice the anchovies in half lengthwise to create twelve pieces of anchovy.
2. Combine the ricotta, mozzarella, Pecorino Romano, egg, salt, and pepper in a medium bowl.
3. Gently spoon the filling into each zucchini flower, filling each one about half full. Then take each anchovy piece and press it down into the center of the filling. Close each flower by gently twisting together the ends.
4. *To fry:* Heat up the oil in a large, tall stock pot over high heat.
5. *To make the batter:* While the oil is heating up, add the flour, salt, and sugar to a large bowl. Gently pour a stream of the sparkling water into the flour, whisking as you go to remove lumps and fully incorporate the liquid and flour. Add a little at a time until it becomes a creamy, clump-free batter that runs from a spoon like a ribbon.
6. Test the oil by dropping a small bit of batter in to see if it bubbles up. If yes, then it's ready. It should be at a temperature between 350 and 360°F (180 and 185°C).
7. Dip two or three stuffed zucchini flowers into the batter and then carefully place them into the hot oil. You do not need to coat the flowers in a thick layer of batter. A light dipping is enough, gently tapping off the excess. (We only fry two or three at a time to prevent crowding the pan.)
8. Once they are crisp and a pale golden color on all sides, 2 to 3 minutes, gently remove them with a slotted spoon and place them on a paper towel-lined surface to drain. Repeat with the remaining zucchini flowers.

TIP

We grow zucchini in our garden each year, so it's easy for us to source these delicate blooms. However, if you don't have the ability to garden, or access to a friend's garden, it's often possible to find zucchini flowers in season at a local farmer's market. Make sure to source the largest and most open blooms that you can.

antipasti e contorni

Caponata

Sicilian Eggplant Relish

. . .

4 servings

The first time I ever had caponata was in Erice, a fairy-tale hilltop town in Sicily where the air smells like fresh pastries and the sea breeze. For some reason, I'd always assumed caponata was served warm, like a vegetable stew. Imagine my surprise when it arrived at our table and I took a bite and was greeted with a cold but unbelievably rich and flavorful dish.

Caponata is a quintessential Sicilian appetizer: sweet, tangy, and salty all at once. It's made with eggplant, tomatoes, olives, capers, and celery, all simmered down in a vinegar-and-tomato base. Here, it's all about the balance of flavors. There are dozens of regional versions, but this is ours. Serve it cold or room temperature with crusty Italian bread and be prepared when everyone asks for seconds.

2 lbs (907 g) eggplant
3 tbsp xtra virgin olive oil, divided
¼ cup (30 g) pine nuts
1 white onion, thinly sliced
2 celery stalks, thinly sliced
½ lb (227 g) pitted green olives, halved
2 vine-ripened tomatoes, cut into 1-inch (2.5 cm) pieces
2 tbsp capers in brine, drained
Sea salt and pepper, to taste
Shredded basil, for serving

For the sauce:

¼ cup (60 ml) white wine vinegar
2½ tbsp tomato paste
1 tbsp honey

1. Preheat the oven to 400°F (200°C).
2. Clean and cut the eggplant into 1-inch (2.5 cm) cubes. If desired, fill a bowl with cold, salty water, submerge the eggplant cubes, and let them sit for 30 minutes to 1 hour to help remove bitterness. Drain the eggplant cubes, pat dry, and toss with about 2 tablespoons of olive oil and then spread evenly on a baking sheet.
3. Roast for 25 to 30 minutes, until fully cooked and tender.
4. Add the pine nuts to a large sauté pan over medium-low heat and toast for 2 to 3 minutes. Once toasted, remove them from the pan and set aside.
5. Warm the remaining 1 tablespoon of olive oil in the same pan. Add the onion and cook for 5 to 7 minutes, until translucent and golden.
6. Add in the celery and cook until softened and browned, about 8 minutes.
7. Add the pine nuts, olives, tomatoes, and capers. Cover with the lid and cook on low heat for about 20 minutes, stirring occasionally.
8. *Make the sauce:* Meanwhile, whisk together the vinegar, tomato paste, and honey in a small bowl. You can add a splash of water if it's too thick.
9. After the vegetables have cooked for about 20 minutes, add the sauce. Add salt and pepper to taste. Cook for 3 to 4 minutes to meld the flavors.
10. Add the roasted eggplant and cook for a few minutes to warm everything through and combine fully.
11. Transfer to a dish or bowl. Cover and let chill in the fridge for at least 2 hours, although overnight is best.
12. Serve cold or at room temperature with some shredded basil.

antipasti e contorni

Peperonata

Stewed Vegetables

. . .

4 servings

If our kitchen had a "greatest hits" playlist, peperonata would be track one. We make it constantly (at least weekly!) during the summer, and the possibilities with it are endless. Our favorite way to enjoy it is over a plate of pasta, but we also use it to top sandwiches or eat it as a side and scoop it up with a slice of bread. It's one of those magical dishes that has rustic flair but also feels rich and luxurious at the same time.

Made with a mix of bell peppers, zucchini, eggplant, tomatoes, onion, and garlic, peperonata is gently cooked until everything breaks down to a silky, jammy blend of veggies. The longer it cooks, the more the flavors deepen, making it the kind of dish that tastes just as good the next day. This is truly one of our favorite things to cook—not just because it's simple and satisfying, but because it feels like you get a bit of summer in every bite.

1 large eggplant
1 to 2 tbsp extra virgin olive oil
½ yellow onion, roughly chopped
2 garlic cloves, quartered
1 large zucchini
1 green bell pepper
1 orange bell pepper
1 red bell pepper
1 yellow bell pepper
Sea salt, to taste
2 vine-ripened tomatoes

1. Clean and cut the eggplant into 1-inch (2.5 cm) cubes. If desired, fill a bowl with cold, salty water, submerge the eggplant cubes, and let them sit for 30 minutes to 1 hour to help remove bitterness. Once finished, drain and set aside.
2. Heat the olive oil in a large sauté pan over medium-low heat. Add the onion and garlic and cook for 5 to 6 minutes, until golden.
3. Halve the zucchini lengthwise, cut into ¼ inch (6 mm) thick slices, and add them to the pan.
4. Chop the peppers into 1-to2-inch (2.5 to 5 cm) pieces and add them to the pan.
5. Add the eggplant, as well as salt to taste. Cover the pan, reduce the heat to low, and cook for 1½ hours. Make sure to stir occasionally to prevent burning. (See Note.)
6. After 1½ hours, roughly chop the tomatoes into about 1-inch (2.5 cm) pieces. Add the tomatoes, stir, and cook for about 30 minutes, until the tomatoes break down, the vegetables soften, and the liquid evaporates, forming a jammy sauce.
7. Remove from the heat and serve. Our favorite way to serve is over pasta, but peperonata is also wonderful as a side, on a sandwich, or over rice.

NOTE

If the vegetables are out of season, they will have less water to release as they cook. If needed, you can add a splash of water here and there to help the vegetables cook and not dry out.

antipasti e contorni

Insalata di Patate

Italian Potato Salad

. . .

4 servings

There are a lot of ways to make potato salad and even more opinions on what makes one "authentically" Italian. Alessio likes to remind me that the recipe for "patate lesse," simple boiled potatoes that are dressed with olive oil or lemon, is technically the traditional version. But in our house, this summery take is what we've always called "potato salad."

It's the kind of side dish that Alessio would throw together for lunch when it is too hot to cook anything else. Just boiled potatoes, excellent olive oil, a splash of high-quality balsamic vinegar, salt, and pepper. Again, the quality of the ingredients matters here.

1 lb (454 g) small red potatoes
Extra virgin olive oil
Balsamic vinegar (the higher the quality, the better)
Sea salt and pepper, to taste
Fresh chopped parsley, for serving

1 Add the potatoes to a large stockpot of salted water over high heat. Bring to a boil and cook the potatoes for 15 to 20 minutes, until fork tender.
2 Drain the potatoes and rinse under cold water to help them cool. You can either remove the peel or leave it on based on your preference.
3 Chop the potatoes into bite-size pieces, about 1-inch (2.5 cm) cubes.
4 Toss the potatoes in a large bowl with a drizzle of olive oil, balsamic vinegar, and salt and pepper to taste.
5 Sprinkle with chopped parsley and serve immediately, or let cool in the fridge first.

antipasti e contorni

Verdure al Forno

Oven-Roasted Vegetables

. . .

4 servings

This isn't a flashy recipe, but it's one we come back to again and again. It's the perfect thing when we're craving something wholesome, healthy, and full of flavor. Verdure al Forno is as simple as it sounds—a medley of chopped vegetables, tossed with olive oil, salt, and herbs and roasted in the oven until golden and caramelized.

We usually make this when we're leaning into healthy eating and need a solid side dish that goes with just about anything. What keeps us coming back, though, are the flavors that roasting brings out—the sweetness of the carrots, the nuttiness of the potatoes—every vegetable becomes addictive in roasted form.

1 lb (454 g) yellow potatoes
2 or 3 large carrots
1 red or orange bell pepper
1 large zucchini
8 asparagus spears
½ red onion
4 garlic cloves
2 tbsp extra virgin olive oil
2 sprigs rosemary
Sea salt and pepper, to taste
Freshly grated Parmigiano Reggiano (optional)

1. Preheat the oven to 400°F (200°C).
2. Wash and dry the potatoes, carrots, pepper, zucchini, and asparagus. Peel the potatoes, carrots, and onion and remove the tough ends from the bottom of the asparagus. Chop all of the vegetables into small, equal pieces, about 1 inch (2.5 cm). Leave the garlic cloves in their skins.
3. Grease a baking sheet with the olive oil.
4. Spread the chopped vegetables evenly along the tray, tossing them a bit to help coat them with the oil. Place the garlic cloves and rosemary sprigs around the pan.
5. Sprinkle everything with salt and pepper to taste. Optionally, you can sprinkle a generous layer of grated Parmigiano Reggiano over the top before baking for added flavor.
6. Bake for 30 to 35 minutes, testing the vegetables with a fork. Everything should be caramelized; the potatoes and carrots should be soft.

antipasti e contorni

Grissini

Thin Italian Breadsticks

...

10 servings, 30 to 40 pieces total

If you've ever sat down at a restaurant in Italy, you've probably seen them—those long, skinny breadsticks sitting in a little basket or standing up out of a vase like a bouquet. Grissini are the most common breadstick in Italy: crispy, crunchy, golden, and well ... addictive. Alessio and I always find ourselves snacking on them while waiting for our food, but they are just as essential at aperitivo hour.

These are nothing like the fluffy, garlic-buttered breadsticks you find at chain restaurants in the US. They are delicate, crunchy, and perfect for nibbling. They originate from the Piedmont region, but now you'll find them all across Italy, from fancy restaurants to rustic trattorias.

- 3¾ tbsp extra virgin olive oil, divided, plus more for greasing
- 1¼ cups (300 ml) warm water
- 2 tsp honey
- 1¾ tsp active dry yeast
- 4 cups (480 g) bread flour, plus more for work surface
- 2½ tsp sea salt
- ½ cup (84 g) fine semolina flour, plus more for rolling

1. Grease a baking sheet with olive oil and set aside.
2. Whisk the water, honey, and yeast together in a large bowl. Let the mixture sit for 10 to 15 minutes, until activated and bubbly.
3. Mix in 1¾ tablespoons of olive oil and then add the bread flour and salt. Combine until a loose dough is formed.
4. Place the dough onto a clean, very lightly floured work surface. (You don't want to incorporate too much extra flour.) Knead the dough to build the gluten. Knead for about 10 minutes, or until smooth and elastic.
5. Place the kneaded dough on the greased baking sheet. Cover with a damp kitchen towel and allow to proof (rise) for 30 minutes.
6. After proofing, use your hands to shape the dough into a rectangle of about 20 × 8 inches (50 × 20 cm). Brush the remaining 2 teaspoons of olive oil all over the top, cover with plastic wrap, and let rise for 1 hour in a warm space.
7. Preheat the oven to 400°F (200°C) and grease two baking sheets with olive oil or line them with parchment paper.
8. Uncover the dough and sprinkle evenly with the semolina flour.
9. Use a sharp knife to cut the dough into about thirty strips, taking care to make them as even in size as possible. They should be roughly ½ inch (1.25 cm) wide and 8 inches (20 cm) long.
10. Lift each strip and gently pull and stretch it to create a long, thin breadstick, about 12 to 14 inches (30 to 36 cm) long. Roll each in a bit of additional semolina flour.
11. Bake for 20 to 25 minutes, until golden, flipping the grissini halfway.
12. Remove from the baking sheet and let them cool on a wire rack. They get crunchier as they cool down!

piatti principali

Insalata di Riso

Cold Rice Salad

. . .

4 servings

The first time I had Insalata di Riso, it was at Alessio's family home, made by his mom, who, like most Italian moms, doesn't use recipes so much as vibes in the kitchen. A handful of this and a bit of that, and somehow it always comes out perfectly. That's the charm of a classic summer dish like this.

There are endless variations of this cold rice salad, and every family has their favorite. Some include tuna; others add cheese cubes or pickled vegetables. This is our take, with sautéed zucchini, sweet corn, colored bell peppers, tomatoes, and olives. You can keep it vegetarian or add in pancetta or chopped wurstel (a German frankfurter), depending on what you have in the fridge. It's easy and bright and the perfect thing to eat on a hot summer day.

- 1¼ cups (250 g) dry long-grain rice
- 1 large zucchini
- ½ red bell pepper
- ½ yellow bell pepper
- 1 tbsp extra virgin olive oil, plus more for drizzling
- 1 cup (150 g) frozen corn, thawed
- 1 cup (150 g) frozen peas, thawed
- 10 cherry tomatoes
- ¼ cup (37 g) pitted black olives
- Pancetta (optional)
- Wurstel (optional)
- 4 or 5 fresh basil leaves, torn
- Sea salt and pepper, to taste

1. Prepare the rice by boiling a large pot of salted water over high heat, cooking the rice according to the package instructions (typically 15 to 18 minutes), and draining off the excess water. Set the rice aside in a bowl to cool.
2. Clean and chop the zucchini and peppers into small pieces, about ½ inch (1.25 cm).
3. Heat the olive oil in a large pan over medium heat.
4. Add the zucchini and peppers to the pan and cook until softened, 8 to 10 minutes.
5. Add in the corn and peas, cooking for an additional 3 to 4 minutes, until warmed through.
6. Meanwhile, slice the tomatoes in half and slice the olives into rings.
7. If using, cook and chop up the pancetta and/or wurstel separately.
8. After the vegetables are cooked, set them aside to cool.
9. Once the rice and vegetables are fully cooled, mix them together in a large bowl. Add the tomatoes and olives, the pancetta and/or wurstel (if using), a drizzle of olive oil, the torn basil leaves, and salt and pepper.
10. Mix everything well and then place in the fridge for at least 1 hour to develop the flavors.

piatti principali

Pasta alla Sonia

Pasta with Tuna and Caper Sauce

. . .

2 servings

This recipe will always have a piece of my heart and a very proud place in this cookbook. It was the first dish that Alessio's mom ever taught me to make. But there's a twist to this story: I told her I hated tuna.

I said it plainly. I didn't like the smell, didn't like the taste, and didn't think that eating it in pasta was for me. But she just smiled and said, "That's because you haven't had my tuna." And with that, she pulled out a can of Italian tuna and began cooking, motioning for me to join her. I watched as she showed me how to combine the capers, olives, and tomato passata. I was supportive, unsure if I'd actually end up enjoying it. I was going to eat it, of course. I would never want to offend her, but actually like tuna? The chances were slim. But when it was ready and I took the first bite of sauce straight from the pot, she was absolutely right. It was rich and comforting and had none of the fishy flavor I had dreaded. I was hooked and shoveled down two helpings.

This recipe is named after her, not because she changed my mind about tuna, but because she did it with love, warmth, and patience. That's the heart of Italian cooking, and now every time I eat pasta with tuna and caper sauce, I'm instantly transported back to her kitchen, standing by her side and learning from a pro.

7 oz (200 g) dry whole wheat pasta
1 tbsp extra virgin olive oil
1 yellow onion, diced
1 garlic clove, peeled and crushed
14 oz (400 g) tomato passata
One 6.3-oz (180 g) can tuna in oil, drained
2 tbsp pitted black olives, halved
1 tbsp capers in brine, drained
Sea salt, to taste
2 anchovies in oil, drained (optional)

1. Bring a large pot of salted water to a boil over high heat and cook the pasta according to the package instructions.
2. Meanwhile, warm the olive oil in a large sauté pan over medium-low heat, add the onion and garlic, and cook for 5 to 7 minutes, until soft and golden.
3. Add the tomato passata and cook for 4 to 5 minutes, stirring to combine.
4. Add the tuna, olives, capers, and a pinch of salt. Optionally, you can add two anchovies as well. If you do this, don't add the salt, as the anchovies are already salty. Cook for 5 minutes, stirring to mix all of the ingredients.
5. Once the pasta is cooked, drain it and add it to the tuna mixture. Stir to combine and serve immediately.

piatti principali

Spaghetti al Pomodoro

Spaghetti with Tomato Sauce

. . .

2 servings

"You can't taste the tomato." That's what Alessio always says when he tries one of those overly seasoned, heavy, jarred pasta sauces from the grocery store. To him (and most Italians), sauce should show off the flavor of the tomatoes, not hide it with a ton of garlic powder, dried herbs, and mystery spices.

If there's one dish that captures the heart of Italian cooking, it's Spaghetti al Pomodoro. It's simple and built entirely on good ingredients. No bells, whistles, or sugar added. Just high-quality tomato passata, a little onion, garlic, fresh basil, and olive oil. That's it! For more on passata, we've provided our favorite sources in Sourcing Authentic Italian Ingredients (and Substitutions) in the US (page 16).

This dish is all about restraint. The tomato sauce lightly coats the pasta rather than drowning it. If you make more sauce than the pasta you're eating? It's all good! Put it in the fridge and enjoy it tomorrow. (See Note.) This is one of our favorite weeknight meals—it's quick, inexpensive, and so satisfying that you'll wonder how something this simple can taste this good.

Extra virgin olive oil
¼ yellow onion, diced
1 garlic clove, minced
14 oz (400 g) tomato passata
7 oz (200 g) dry spaghetti
5 or 6 fresh basil leaves
Sea salt, to taste

1. Heat a drizzle of olive oil in a large sauté pan over low heat.
2. Add the onion and garlic to the pan. Cook for 5 to 7 minutes, until softened and golden. Be careful not to burn. Add in the tomato passata. Stir to combine. Simmer the sauce uncovered over low heat until the pasta has finished cooking.
3. Meanwhile, cook the spaghetti in a large pot of salted water according to the package instructions.
4. Drain and return the pasta to the pot. Tear three or four basil leaves and add them to the sauce. Add salt, to taste, and stir to combine.
5. Ladle ⅓ to 1 cup (80 to 240 ml) of sauce from the pan and transfer it to the pot of pasta, stirring to coat the pasta.
6. Divide the pasta between two plates, ladle ⅓ to ½ cup (80 to 120 ml) of sauce over the top of each, and garnish each with more basil.

NOTE

If you're looking for a quick and easy tomato sauce to pair with another recipe, this one is perfect. Simply adjust the ingredients for the amount of servings you need.

piatti principali

Pasta ai Peperoni di Alessio

Alessio's Pepper Pasta

. . .

4 servings

This is one of our ultimate comfort dishes. We make it all the time, and it never lets us down. In fact, we always think one plate is never enough. It's creamy and deeply flavorful, but here's the twist—there's no cream involved at all. The magic comes entirely from the peppers.

The sauce is made by slowly cooking down yellow and orange bell peppers with onion, garlic, and just a touch of butter and olive oil. As they simmer, the peppers release their natural sweetness and moisture, slowly transforming into a soft, silky sauce that clings to every inch of pasta. It's rich without being heavy and perfect on any long pasta you love. We call it Alessio's Pepper Pasta because, well ... it's his specialty. He perfected it over time, and now it's one of those recipes we crave on long days and lazy weekends.

Extra virgin olive oil

½ tbsp unsalted butter

½ yellow onion, thinly sliced

1 garlic clove, quartered

3 yellow bell peppers, seeded and thinly sliced

2 orange bell peppers, seeded and thinly sliced

Sea salt, to taste

11 oz (320 g) dry long pasta (spaghetti, tagliatelle, pappardelle, etc.)

1. Warm up a drizzle of olive oil and the butter in a large pan over low heat. Heat until the butter is melted.
2. Add the onion and garlic and stir. Cook for 5 to 7 minutes, until golden.
3. Add the peppers to the pan and season with a bit of salt. Cover the pan and cook for 90 minutes, stirring occasionally to prevent burning and to cook evenly. Add splashes of water as needed to prevent drying out. The peppers will be finished when they have released all of their water and it has evaporated. You should be left with very soft, silky peppers and a smooth, creamy sauce.
4. Bring a large pot of salted water to a boil and cook the pasta according to the package instructions. Once finished, drain the pasta and add it to the pan of peppers. Stir to combine and then serve.

piatti principali

Spaghetti alla Vongole

Spaghetti with Clams

. . .

4 servings

This one belongs to Alessio. He absolutely adores Spaghetti alla Vongole, a dish that's as coastal Italian as it gets. When he first told me how much he loves it, I was skeptical. Not only because I'm not a huge seafood fan, but because I'm actually allergic to shellfish. So this is one recipe that I admire from a safe distance, while Alessio lights up whenever it hits his plate.

His hometown in Northern Italy is only about an hour away from Venice, which means incredibly fresh seafood is never far. And in this dish, the freshness of the clams makes all the difference. The sauce is incredibly simple: olive oil, garlic, parsley, and a hint of heat from pepperoncino. Alessio says the flavors that come together are pure magic. This is a classic summer pasta for coastal Italians. Just one rule: no cheese. Seriously. Alessio says it's a non-negotiable.

2 lbs (907 g) fresh clams
1 tbsp cornmeal
11 oz (320 g) dry spaghetti
½ cup (120 ml) extra virgin olive oil
2 garlic cloves, minced
1 dried red Calabrian chili pepper, deseeded and cut into thirds
Sea salt and pepper, to taste
Handful of fresh parsley, chopped

1. Clean the clams, throwing away any that are broken. Place them in a large bowl of cold water with the cornmeal for 30 minutes to 1 hour. Rinse and drain to remove any sand.
2. Bring a large pot of salted water to a boil and cook the spaghetti according to the package instructions.
3. Meanwhile, warm up the olive oil in a large pan over low heat. Once warmed, add the garlic and chili pepper. Cook for about 1 minute, until fragrant.
4. Increase the heat to medium and add in the clams, stirring to coat them in the oil, garlic, and Calabrian chili pepper. Be careful not to scratch your pan with the clam shells!
5. Add salt and pepper to taste, as well as the parsley, and toss to gently coat the clams again.
6. Cover the pan and cook for about 3 minutes, until the clams open. Discard any that do not open.
7. Drain the pasta when it is finished cooking, reserving ⅓ to ½ cup (80 to 120 ml) of pasta water and add both the pasta and the reserved pasta water to the pan with the clams. Toss to coat and combine.
8. Serve immediately with a bit more chopped parsley, but no cheese. (we're serious!)

piatti principali

Pasta Amore

Pasta with Olives, Tomato, and Smoked Ricotta

. . .

2 servings

If Pasta ai Peperoni di Alessio (Alessio's Pepper Pasta, page 111) is his signature dish, then this one is mine. I first tasted something like it at a restaurant in Lierna, a charming little town on Lake Como. It was one of those meals where everything felt perfect. The view, the breeze, and then … the pasta. It arrived with whole wheat spaghetti (which surprised me) and a combination of olives, cherry tomatoes, and smoked ricotta. I loved it so much I took a picture of the plate right then and there.

The recipe wasn't broken down on the menu, so I came home determined to recreate it myself. And after some trial and error, we ended up with this dish—a mix of ingredients and memories we'll never forget. It's fresh, savory, a little smoky, and a love letter to that summer day on Lake Como.

- Sea salt, to taste
- 5½ oz (160 g) dry whole wheat spaghetti
- 1½ cups (165 g) fresh cherry tomatoes
- Extra virgin olive oil
- ¼ yellow onion, diced
- 1 garlic clove, minced
- ½ cup (74 g) pitted black olives, sliced
- Handful of fresh basil leaves
- 1 cup (170 g) shredded smoked ricotta (can sub with another smoked cheese, if desired)

1. Bring a large pot of salted water to a boil and cook the pasta according to the package instructions.
2. In the meantime, halve the cherry tomatoes.
3. Heat a generous drizzle of olive oil in a large sauté pan over low heat and add the onion and garlic. Cook for 4 to 5 minutes, until golden.
4. Add the tomatoes and olives into the pan, cooking for 7 to 8 minutes, until the tomatoes are softened. You do not need to fully cook down the tomatoes. They should still hold a bit of shape.
5. Once the pasta is cooked, drain and add it into the pan. Tear the basil leaves, add them in, and stir to combine. Cook for 1 minute, or until the basil is wilted, and then plate the pasta.
6. Top with a generous amount of shredded smoked ricotta.

piatti principali

Cacio e Pepe

• • •

2 servings

When we were traveling in Rome, we stumbled upon the best plate of carbonara we'd ever tasted. Alessio and I still dream about it. But I have to confess that I actually fell head over heels for a second Roman pasta: Cacio e Pepe. It's creamy, peppery, and perfectly salty, and it somehow manages to feel like a warm hug, despite being made from only three ingredients: pasta, Pecorino Romano, and black pepper.

This dish is a master class in restraint. No cream, no butter, no garlic—just traditional, time-honored technique. It's about building the sauce by emulsifying cheese and pasta water, and it requires a little patience and stirring. The result is 100% worth it. Alessio might always vote for carbonara, but for me, Cacio e Pepe will always win. Once you try it, it just might become your favorite, too.

- 7 oz (200 g) dry spaghetti or tonnarelli pasta
- ½ tbsp freshly cracked black pepper, plus more for serving
- 4½ oz (127 g) freshly grated Pecorino Romano, plus more for serving

1. Bring a large pot of salted water to a boil and cook the pasta to al dente according to the package instructions. Drain the pasta but reserve the pasta water. Don't throw it out! You can keep it warming on the stove over low heat.
2. Heat the pepper for about 30 seconds in a large sauté pan over low heat to bring out the aroma and toast the pepper. Stir to toast evenly.
3. Ladle ⅔ to 1 cup (160 to 240 ml) of pasta water into the pan of pepper. Immediately add the pasta to the pan and stir continuously to keep the noodles from sticking. If the pan is too dry, ladle in another ⅓ to ½ cup (80 to 120 ml) of pasta water. You can keep doing this if the water evaporates.
4. In a small bowl, combine half of the Pecorino Romano with another ⅓ to ½ cup (80 to 120 ml) of pasta water. Whisk vigorously.
5. Add the remaining Pecorino Romano and whisk again. You'll have to eyeball the ratio of pasta water to cheese here. You want a creamy sauce that doesn't have any lumps. Add a little bit more water or cheese as needed to get this consistency.
6. As you are whisking, hold the bowl of cream sauce over the pan of spaghetti to help bring it back up to temperature before adding it to the pan. Remove the pan from the heat and pour in the sauce, stirring continuously to blend everything together.
7. Let sit for about 1 minute before plating the pasta and topping with cracked black pepper and some additional grated Pecorino Romano.

piatti principali

Pasta Fredda Mediterranea

Mediterranean Pasta Salad

...

2 servings

We went back and forth on this one. There are so many versions of Pasta Fredda, some packed with grilled vegetables, others loaded with tuna, beans, or more elaborate dressings. But in the end, we kept coming back to this: the Mediterranean version. It's simple, classic, and exactly what you crave on a hot summer day.

With cherry tomatoes, fresh mozzarella, black olives, basil, and a good drizzle of olive oil, this cold pasta salad is light, refreshing, and full of flavor. It's perfect for picnics, family reunions, beach days, or those stifling afternoons when the thought of turning on the oven makes you want to cry.

This is a dish we make when we want something satisfying without much effort. Remember, when a recipe is simple, it's all about high-quality ingredients. Grab the juicy and ripe summer tomatoes, the fresh mozzarella, and the good olive oil. You'll soon realize that the simplest things really are the best.

- 5½ oz (160 g) dry mezze maniche pasta (or your preferred small pasta shape)
- 2 cups (420 g) fresh cherry tomatoes
- Sea salt, to taste
- 7 oz (200 g) fresh mozzarella, cubed
- ¾ cup (112 g) pitted black olives, whole or sliced
- Extra virgin olive oil
- 5 or 6 small basil leaves

1. Bring a large pot of salted water to a boil and cook the pasta according to the package instructions.
2. In the meantime, wash and prepare the cherry tomatoes by cutting them into quarters and sprinkling them with salt. Set aside.
3. When the pasta is al dente, drain and rinse with cold water to help cool the pasta.
4. Once drained, put the pasta into a large bowl. Add the tomatoes, mozzarella, and olives. Drizzle with olive oil and then tear the basil leaves and sprinkle them into the pasta. Stir to combine. Serve.

piatti principali

Gnudi di Ricotta e Spinaci

Spinach Ricotta Dumplings

. . .

4 servings

If you love gnocchi, you're going to love gnudi. The name actually means "naked" in Italian, and the idea is that these delicious bites are naked ravioli (without the pasta). You get all the good stuff: ricotta, spinach, Parmigiano Reggiano, and a hint of nutmeg, rolled into precious little dumplings and tossed in a butter and sage sauce.

The first time I had gnudi was in Valdobbiadene, a beautiful town tucked into the hills of prosecco country. Their version was a little bit different from this one (it was autumn at the time), but I still remember being shocked by that first bite: pillowy, rich, and comforting. It was one of those meals that lingers with you, even on the flight home. This version is a great place to start if you've never made gnudi before. It's simple and surprisingly light, even with all the cheese and butter.

For the gnudi:

12½ oz (354 g) ricotta

½ cup (60 g) all-purpose flour, plus more for dusting

Extra virgin olive oil

1½ lbs (680 g) fresh spinach

1½ oz (42 g) freshly grated Parmigiano Reggiano

1 large egg, lightly beaten

¼ tsp ground nutmeg

Sea salt and pepper, to taste

For the sauce:

4 tbsp unsalted butter

7 or 8 fresh sage leaves, chopped

Grated Parmigiano Reggiano

Special Equipment

Fine-mesh strainer

1. *To make the gnudi:* Place the ricotta in a fine-mesh strainer and allow it to drain over a bowl for at least 30 minutes. The longer the better, as you want the ricotta to be as dry as possible.
2. Lightly flour a tray or plate and set aside.
3. Heat a drizzle of olive oil in a large sauté pan over low heat and add the spinach. Allow it to cook uncovered over low heat, stirring occasionally, until wilted, 2 to 4 minutes.
4. Remove the spinach from the heat and drain it. Allow the spinach to cool a bit before using your hands or a towel to squeeze out as much water as possible. Again, you want the spinach to be as dry as possible.
5. Finely chop the spinach.
6. Combine the spinach, ricotta, Parmigiano Reggiano, flour, egg, nutmeg, salt, and pepper in a large bowl. Mix well to fully combine.
7. Form the gnudi by rolling 1-inch (2.5 cm) balls of the mixture between your hands. Place the balls on the prepared tray and use your fingers to gently flatten each ball just a bit.
8. Bring a large pot of salted water to a boil.
9. *To make the sauce:* Meanwhile, melt the butter in a large sauté pan over low heat and add the sage, stirring to coat the leaves.
10. Add the gnudi to the boiling water. They should rise to the surface when they are ready, and it should take only a few minutes.
11. Immediately drain the gnudi and add them to the pan with the butter and sage sauce. Gently stir them to coat.
12. Serve immediately with a sprinkle of grated Parmigiano Reggiano on top.

piatti principali

Pasini Pizza

. . .

4 servings

This recipe was born out of desperation—and love. Alessio missed the pizza from back home in Italy. No matter how many restaurants we tried or frozen pizzas we ordered (even ones shipped straight from Italy), nothing quite hit the spot. The crust was always too thick, too bready, too far from that perfect crispy yet chewy bite you get from a real Italian pizzeria. So … we decided to make our own.

Now, before you panic at the thought of making homemade pizza dough—especially if the word "knead" makes you break out into a cold sweat—don't worry! This recipe is totally doable. In fact, I was scared, too, at first, and it took us quite a few tries to get it right. Now it's our weekend tradition. It's a dough that makes us feel like we're back in Alessio's hometown, even though we're baking right in our standard oven here in the US (no fancy pizza oven or tools required). Every Friday we make this dough, and every Saturday and Sunday night we're sliding hot pizzas from sheet pans and topping them with our favorites.

Our go-to is classic: tomato passata, mozzarella, Parmigiano Reggiano, a sprinkle of oregano, and a final topping of hand-shredded mozzarella di bufala after baking. But this dough is a blank canvas, and you can make it your own. Actually—we feel obligated to say one thing: Don't put pineapple on this dough.

That said, we've included a few of our favorite topping combinations at the end of the recipe: from white pizza and veggie, to classics like quattro stagioni. Once you master this recipe, you'll never go back to store-bought frozen pizza again. It might just become a weekend tradition of your own.

- 2 cups (250 g) all-purpose flour, plus more for kneading
- 2 cups (250 g) whole wheat flour
- ¾ tsp (2 g) active dry yeast
- About 1⅔ cups (375 to 400 ml) warm water, divided
- 4 tsp (20 ml) extra virgin olive oil
- 2½ tsp (15 to 16 g) sea salt
- Fine semolina flour, for dusting
- Toppings of choice (see Our Favorite Pizza Topping Combinations)

Special Equipment

Airtight container

NOTE

The temperature of your home makes a difference in the rise of the dough. The optimal temperature is 75°F (24°C); however, if your home is colder, allow for additional time to rise.

1. Whisk together the all-purpose flour and whole wheat flour in a large bowl until thoroughly combined.
2. Mix the yeast with approximately ¼ cup (60 ml) of the warm water in a small cup. Whisk until dissolved and let sit for 15 minutes to activate.
3. Add the remaining warm water to the flour mixture and stir to combine. It's okay if there are still some dry flour bits, as we will be adding more moisture shortly.
4. After 15 minutes, pour the activated yeast mixture into the flour mixture. Stir to combine.
5. Add in the olive oil and salt and mix with a spoon or your hands until a loose dough forms.
6. Transfer the dough to a floured work surface. Knead for 5 to 10 minutes, adding flour or water as needed to achieve the desired consistency. When finished, the dough should be soft, pliable, and easily kneaded, and it shouldn't stick to your hands.
7. Shape the dough into a ball and return it to the mixing bowl. Cover the bowl with plastic wrap to prevent air from entering, using a rubber band around the edge to lock it in. Let it rest at room temperature for 5 to 7 hours, until doubled in size. (See Note.)
8. After proofing, place the dough in the fridge overnight.

9 The next day, 3 to 3½ hours before baking, divide the dough into four equal balls, approximately 7.8 to 8.5 ounces (220 to 240 g) each. Using your hands, gently fold the dough balls in on themselves to create a taut surface across the top. The action is similar to how a mozzarella ball is formed. Make sure to pinch the bottom closed to seal.

10 Allow them to rest on the counter in an airtight container until ready to bake. This recipe should yield four dough balls, so if you are baking only two pizzas, place the remaining balls in an airtight container and put them back into the fridge until the next day.

11 When ready to bake, preheat the oven to 500°F (260°C). Take each ball and roll it in a bit of semolina flour, so it is no longer sticky.

12 Shape and stretch each dough ball into your desired pizza form. We typically make more of a "pizza Romana" style, which has a thinner outer crust than pizza Napoletana.

13 Top with your favorite ingredients. (We wait to add the mozzarella until the last few minutes of cooking to prevent burning, since it takes longer to bake the crust in a conventional oven than it does in a brick pizza oven.)

14 Place the pizzas on sheet pans that have been dusted with a bit of semolina flour and bake for 11 to 13 minutes, until the edges are golden brown. Check the oven temperature after opening to make sure the heat is still 500°F (260°C). If not, increase the heat. Opening the oven often causes heat to escape, and you want to keep it as hot as possible.

15 After baking, add any additional toppings and serve.

Our Favorite Pizza Topping Combinations

THE CLASSIC

Top the pizza with tomato passata, a generous amount of grated Parmigiano Reggiano, and oregano before placing it in the oven. In the last few minutes of baking, sprinkle on some hand-shredded, fresh mozzarella and basil leaves. After baking, top with additional hand-torn mozzarella di bufala.

WHITE PIZZA

Brush olive oil over the entire surface of the pizza dough and top with a generous amount of grated Parmigiano Reggiano before placing in the oven. In the last few minutes of baking, sprinkle on some hand-torn, fresh mozzarella. After baking, top with additional hand-torn mozzarella di bufala, fresh arugula, and freshly cracked black pepper.

QUATTRO STAGIONI "THE FOUR SEASONS"

Top the pizza with tomato passata, a generous amount of grated Parmigiano Reggiano, and oregano. Next you will divide your pizza toppings by quarter, representing the four seasons. In one corner, place sliced black olives; in the next, place strips of prosciutto; the next will have sliced artichoke hearts; and the final quarter will have sliced mushrooms. In the last few minutes of baking, sprinkle on some hand-torn, fresh mozzarella.

VEGGIE

Top your pizza with tomato passata, a generous amount of grated Parmigiano Reggiano, and a mixture of freshly cooked vegetables. Some of our favorites include asparagus, peppers, eggplant, zucchini, radicchio, black olives, and corn. Make sure your vegetables are precooked before baking the pizza. In the last few minutes of baking, sprinkle on some hand-torn, fresh mozzarella.

SUN-DRIED TOMATOES

Brush olive oil over the entire surface of the pizza dough and top with a generous amount of grated Parmigiano Reggiano. Add drained sun-dried tomatoes and black olives. In the last few minutes of baking, sprinkle on some shredded smoked ricotta, hand-torn, fresh mozzarella, and basil leaves. After baking, top with additional hand-torn mozzarella di bufala.

Polpette

Meatballs

. . .

4 servings

Let's clear something up: In Italy, you won't find giant meatballs sitting on top of a heaping plate of spaghetti. That iconic image is 100% Italian American, and while we respect the comfort it brings, that's not how these Polpette are traditionally served in Italy.

In Italy, meatballs are usually served as a second course (a "secondo") on their own with a bit of sauce or a side of vegetables. They're smaller, more tender, and simmered in a delicious simple sauce. If Italians do add meatballs to pasta, they're usually tiny, like the size of marbles. So the next time you're tempted to plop a baseball-size meatball onto a plate of spaghetti, remember what we told you.

This version is Alessio's favorite kind—soft, flavorful, and packed with Parmigiano Reggiano, parsley, and breadcrumbs for the perfect texture. This recipe might just change the way you think about meatballs forever.

For the meatballs:

1 lb (454 g) ground beef

1 oz (28 g) grated Parmigiano Reggiano

1 large egg, beaten

½ cup (120 ml) milk

1 tbsp chopped parsley

Sea salt, to taste

1 cup (120 g) dry breadcrumbs

For the sauce:

1 to 2 tbsp extra virgin olive oil

1 large carrot, chopped

½ yellow onion, chopped

½ cup (120 ml) red wine

One 24½-oz (700 g) jar tomato passata

Sea salt, to taste

1. *To make the meatballs:* Combine the beef, Parmigiano Reggiano, egg, milk, parsley, and salt in a large bowl. Mix well.
2. Add the breadcrumbs, a little at a time, stirring until fully combined.
3. Once everything is mixed, begin forming meatballs by rolling small amounts of the mixture between your hands. You want to make them just a bit smaller than the size of a golf ball. No larger! Set them aside while you prepare the sauce. (See Note.)
4. *To make the sauce:* Warm the olive oil in a large sauté pan over medium-low heat.
5. Add the carrot and onion to the oil. Cook for 7 to 8 minutes, until soft.
6. Add the meatballs to the pan and cook, turning occasionally, until browned, 8 to 10 minutes. Add the red wine.
7. Cook, uncovered, until the wine evaporates, then add the tomato passata and season with salt. Cover and cook for 20 to 25 minutes, stirring occasionally, until the sauce thickens and the meatballs are cooked through.
8. Once finished, you can serve as is or, if you prefer a heartier meal, remove the meatballs from the sauce and use the sauce on top of your favorite pasta as a "primo." Then, serve the meatballs by themselves as a "secondo" with a salad.

NOTE

If you want a creamier sauce, you can roll the meatballs in a light dusting of flour before cooking them in the pan.

piatti principali

Parmigiana di Melanzane

Eggplant Parmigiana

. . .

6 servings

Before we dive into this recipe, let's clear up a delicious little misconception: This is not eggplant Parmesan the way most Americans know it. You won't find thick rounds of eggplant, breaded and deep fried, under a load of melted mozzarella and marinara here. Instead, this is the Italian version: Parmigiana di Melanzane, which you can think of it like an eggplant lasagna with the eggplant playing the role of the lasagna noodles.

It's all about the layers. Thin slices of eggplant are stacked with a simple passata sauce, cubes of fresh mozzarella, torn basil, and of course, Parmigiano Reggiano. Then everything is baked until bubbling and golden. It's a rustic dish that's perfect for summertime when eggplants are everywhere. It gets better with time, so we always eat half of it for dinner the first day and pop the rest in the fridge to enjoy later on. It's Italian comfort food at its finest.

Extra virgin olive oil
1 yellow onion, chopped
35 oz (1 kg) tomato passata
Sea salt and pepper, to taste
1 cup (20 g) loosely packed, small, fresh basil leaves
1 lb (454 g) mozzarella
4 lbs (1.8 kg) eggplant
5 oz (142 g) grated Parmigiano Reggiano

Special Equipment
Fine-mesh strainer
9 × 13-inch (23 × 33 cm) baking dish

1 Heat a generous amount of olive oil in a large sauté pan over medium-low heat.

2 Once the oil is warm, add the onion to the pan. Cook for 5 to 7 minutes, until softened and golden. Take care not to burn the onion.

3 Add the tomato passata, and season with a bit of salt and pepper, and a few of the basil leaves. Add a bit of water to the passata jar to loosen any remaining sauce and pour it into the pan.

4 Cook uncovered for 1 hour over low heat, stirring occasionally to prevent burning. Meanwhile, preheat the oven to 400°F (200°C).

5 Cut about three-quarters of the mozzarella into small cubes, about ½ inch (1.25 cm). If needed, set aside the cubes in a mesh strainer to drain over a bowl. Shred the remaining mozzarella with your hands and set it aside.

6 Wash the eggplants and cut lengthwise into ⅛-inch (3 mm) slices.

7 Place the eggplant slices on two baking sheets lined with parchment paper. Drizzle the eggplant with olive oil and bake for 20 minutes, or until soft. Be sure to flip them halfway through for even cooking. You might have to do this in batches, as there will be a lot of eggplant slices. Once all eggplant slices have been baked, set them aside.

8 After the sauce is finished and the eggplant slices are baked, you're ready to assemble. Reduce the oven temperature to 350°F (180°C).

9 In a 9 × 13-inch (23 × 33 cm) baking dish, spread a little sauce on the bottom to prevent sticking.

10 Place the first layer of eggplant on the bottom. Spoon some sauce on top to evenly cover the eggplant and then add a layer of the cubed mozzarella. Make sure there aren't any eggplant slices that are not in the sauce.

11 Sprinkle a layer of Parmigiano Reggiano and some torn basil leaves over top.

12 Continue making these layers, rotating the vertical or horizontal direction of the eggplant to fill any empty spaces, until all the eggplant is used. You should have at least three layers.

13 On top, add a final layer of sauce and the hand-shredded mozzarella.

14 Finally, sprinkle with a generous amount of Parmigiano Reggiano.

15 Bake uncovered for 30 to 35 minutes, and broil for an additional 2 to 3 minutes to make the top golden brown and bubbly.

16 Rest for 20 minutes before slicing.

piatti principali

Alessio Panino

Alessio's Best Sandwich

. . .

1 sandwich

We've had some truly unforgettable sandwiches in Italy—one from a walk-up counter in Florence that stopped us in our tracks, and another from a tiny cheese shop in Ortigia that we still dream about. They're layered with bold flavors and just the right textures.

This is Alessio's go-to sandwich when we're back at home and craving something just as delicious. It's filling and full of Mediterranean flavors: mashed avocado, cherry tomatoes, olives, provolone, mozzarella di bufala, fresh herbs, and our not-so-secret weapon—a generous layer of artichoke bruschetta cream. We usually use a store-bought jar by Cucina & Amore, but if you'd rather make your own, feel free to blend some cooked artichoke hearts with olive oil, garlic, fresh parsley, and a little lemon juice until smooth and creamy.

This sandwich is proof that you don't need a plane ticket to Italy to taste something truly special. Just the right bread, some good ingredients, a balance of flavors and textures, and a little inspiration from a hungry Italian husband.

½ avocado
Sea salt and pepper, to taste
6-inch (15 cm) loaf of artisan bread (our favorite is a seeded loaf)
5 cherry tomatoes, halved
2 slices provolone
3 cherry-sized balls of buffalo mozzarella (ciliegine of mozzarella di bufala)
One 7.9-oz (225 g) jar artichoke bruschetta cream (our favorite is Cucina & Amore)
6 kalamata olives, pitted
3 fresh basil leaves
1 sprig thyme
Extra virgin olive oil

1. In a small bowl, mash the avocado with a fork and add a pinch of salt. Stir to combine.
2. Slice the bread in half lengthwise, taking care not to cut all the way through, so the bread opens but is still connected.
3. Slather a layer of mashed avocado on the bottom side of the bread. Press the cherry tomatoes into the avocado.
4. Layer the provolone over the tomatoes.
5. Hand shred the mozzarella and layer over the provolone.
6. Next, on the top side of the bread, spread a generous amount of the artichoke bruschetta cream. Press the olives into the spread.
7. Remove the thyme leaves from the sprig. Place the basil and thyme over the olives.
8. Sprinkle a bit of salt and pepper over the mozzarella. Add a finishing drizzle of olive oil, close up the sandwich, and enjoy.

Torta al Limone e Olio d'Oliva

Olive Oil Lemon Cake

. . .

10 servings

This cake is everything you love about summer desserts—it's light, citrusy, and just sweet enough. It feels effortless and elegant at the same time, and it's perfect to serve at a dinner party or when you're enjoying a little dolce far niente (the sweetness of doing nothing) on a slow afternoon.

We use extra virgin olive oil instead of butter, which gives the cake a rich, velvety crumb and just a hint of fruitiness that pairs beautifully with the brightness of the lemon juice and zest. If you've never baked olive oil cake before, this is the best recipe to start with. It's simple, with no frills, and easy to execute.

This is also one of those cakes that tastes even better the next day, so feel free to make it in advance. Dust it with powdered sugar and serve it as is or add a spoonful of fresh whipped cream and berries if you want to make things fancy.

¾ cup (180 ml) mild extra virgin olive oil, plus more for greasing
2¼ cups (270 g) all-purpose flour
2½ tsp baking powder
Pinch of sea salt
3 large eggs, room temperature
1 cup (200 g) granulated sugar
⅔ cup (160 ml) whole milk
Juice of 1 lemon
Zest of 2 lemons
Powdered sugar, for dusting

Special Equipment
8-inch (20 cm) round cake pan
Electric mixer or stand mixer

1. Preheat the oven to 350°F (180°C). Brush an 8-inch (20 cm) round cake pan with a drizzle of olive oil. Line the bottom of the pan with parchment paper.
2. Sift together the flour, baking powder, and salt in a medium bowl.
3. Beat the eggs and sugar together with an electric mixer in a medium bowl until fluffy and creamy, 3 to 4 minutes.
4. On medium-low speed, continue to beat the batter while slowly drizzling in the olive oil, followed by the milk, lemon juice, and lemon zest.
5. Use a spoon or spatula to fold in the flour mixture, a little bit at a time, taking care to mix until just incorporated. Do not overmix.
6. Pour the batter into the prepared cake pan and bake for 40 to 45 minutes, until it's golden brown on top and a toothpick inserted in the middle comes out clean.
7. Allow to cool in the pan for 10 minutes before moving to a cooling rack to cool completely.
8. Dust with powdered sugar before serving.

Pesche Caramellate

Caramelized Peaches

. . .

2 servings

Warm, juicy peaches baked until tender and topped with a silky vanilla caramel sauce. What more could you want in the summer?

For me, this recipe also hits a little nostalgic note. When I was growing up in the South, peaches were always a big part of summer, and my grandmother made the best peach cobbler I've ever had. The scent of baked peaches still brings me right back to her table. That's why I love this dish—it's the perfect combination of the two cultures I love.

This version is a little more refined than cobbler—more like cobbler's elegant Italian cousin—but the feeling it gives me is just the same. It's homey, sweet, and full of amore. Serve these peaches with a scoop of vanilla ice cream or fresh whipped cream, and it's like summer on your spoon.

4 yellow peaches

½ cup plus 2 tsp (100 g) granulated sugar, divided

2 tbsp water

3 tbsp heavy cream, room temperature

1 tbsp unsalted butter, room temperature

½ tsp vanilla bean paste

Vanilla ice cream or fresh whipped cream, for serving

Special Equipment

8 × 8-inch (20 × 20 cm) square baking dish

1. Preheat the oven to 350°F (180°C).
2. Clean the peaches, cut them in half, remove the pits, and cut them into 1-inch (2.5 cm) slices.
3. Place the peach slices into an 8 × 8-inch (20 × 20 cm) square baking dish and sprinkle with 2 teaspoons of sugar.
4. Bake for 20 to 25 minutes, until the peaches soften and the sugar is melted.
5. Meanwhile, make the caramel by combining the remaining ½ cup (100 g) of sugar and the water in a small saucepan over medium-low heat. Bring to a soft boil while stirring constantly. Continue to cook, without stirring, until the syrup turns a golden amber color, 10 to 20 minutes.
6. Remove from the heat and slowly whisk in the heavy cream.
7. Add the butter and vanilla bean paste, continuing to whisk until smooth and thick, 1 to 2 minutes.
8. Plate the peaches and pour the caramel sauce over the top, adding a scoop of ice cream or whipped cream before serving.

bevande

Spritz Aperol

Traditional Aperol Spritz

. . .

1 serving

If there's one thing Alessio insists on doing right, it's a proper Spritz Aperol. Though he's from Friuli-Venezia Giulia, he's just a stone's throw away from Veneto, home of the original spritz. And when it comes to this iconic Italian aperitivo, let's just say he has some strong opinions.

You'll find a lot of spritz variations out there—some too sweet, some too bitter, some too diluted, and some that swap in club soda instead of sparkling water. According to Alessio (and honestly, he's right!), that's just not how it's supposed to be done. Traditional Italian spritz uses frizzante, or light sparkling water, not club soda, which has added sodium and can interfere with the clean, delicate flavors of the drink.

This is the real version: crisp, slightly bitter, very bright, and perfectly refreshing on a warm summer evening. It's meant to be sipped slowly, ideally with a little bowl of olives or salty potato chips, a gorgeous sunset, and some friends to chat with.

Ice
2 parts Aperol
1 part Prosecco
Splash of sparkling water
Green olives
Orange slice

1. Fill a glass halfway with ice.
2. Add the Aperol and Prosecco.
3. Add a splash of sparkling water (not club soda!) and stir.
4. Garnish with a toothpick of olives and a slice of fresh orange.

bevande

Limoncello Fatto in Casa

Homemade Limoncello

. . .

36 servings, three 16-oz (500 ml) bottles

In Italy, a meal doesn't end with dessert and coffee, it ends with a "digestivo." After a big dinner, especially when dining out with friends, it's common for the restaurant owner to offer a complimentary shot of something strong to help "digest" the meal. It's a small gesture, but one that's full of hospitality and tradition.

One of our favorites is limoncello. It's bright, fragrant, and bursting with lemon flavor (and its sunshine-yellow color always reminds me of long summer evenings in Italy). You'll find bottles of it tucked into freezers across the country, ready to be served ice-cold in tiny little glasses after dinner.

While it's easy to find limoncello at the store, making your own is something special—and gives you some serious bragging rights. The process is simple, but you must be patient as lemon peel is steeped in high-proof alcohol for 30 days and then blended with a simple syrup. It tastes especially good when sipped slowly on a summer evening. And yes, we said "sipped." Limoncello isn't meant to be thrown back like a shot. It's meant to be savored. Take your time and let the flavors linger. It's the perfect ending to a good meal and an even better way to toast summer.

10 small organic lemons

3⅛ cups (750 ml) 190 proof grain alcohol

3¼ cups (650 g) granulated sugar

3⅛ cups (750 ml) water

Special Equipment

2-qt (2 L) airtight jar

2-qt (2 L) saucepan

Fine-mesh sieve

Funnel

Three 16-oz (500 ml) airtight glass bottles

1. Clean and scrub the lemons well. Use a peeler to carefully remove the outer yellow part of the peel, taking care not to get any of the bitter white pith.
2. Place the lemon peel into a 2-quart (2 L) airtight jar.
3. Add the alcohol to the jar.
4. Let the lemon rind steep in a dark, cool place for 1 month. Gently turn and agitate the jar every day or so to help mix the ingredients.
5. After 30 days, combine the sugar and water in a 2-quart (2 L) saucepan over medium heat and stir constantly until the sugar is dissolved.
6. Increase the heat to medium-high and bring the mixture to a boil. Continue boiling for 5 to 7 minutes, allowing some of the water to evaporate and the syrup to thicken. The syrup should be a pale straw color and thick enough to lightly coat the back of a spoon. Do not allow it to darken to amber.
7. Remove the pan from the heat and allow it to cool.
8. In the meantime, use a fine-mesh sieve to strain the jar of lemon-infused alcohol into a large mixing bowl, discarding the solids.
9. When the syrup is completely cool, pour it into the bowl of lemon-infused alcohol. Stir to combine.
10. Use a funnel to pour the liquid into three 16-ounce (500 ml) airtight bottles, and you're ready to enjoy. Serve very cold for the best experience.

Hosting an Italian Dinner Party

Summer dinner parties are where Italian culture really shines. Everything moves outside. The food gets lighter. The spritzes flow. And the table becomes a little slice of joy under the evening sun. Golden light fading into pinks and oranges the color of Aperol? Heavenly.

Here we walk you through how to host your own Italian-inspired summer dinner party, whether you're going full Amalfi Coast or just having a few friends over with string lights and vases of herbs on the table.

. . .

The Vibe

Time: Start around golden hour and let the meal roll into the nighttime.

Setting: Outdoors, if possible. Think string lights, candles (taper and citronella sprinkled around!), a white linen tablecloth, and a playlist of classic Italian love songs.

Energy: Effortless but thoughtful. Big bowls of pasta. Fresh, crusty bread. Clinking glasses. Guests helping to bring platters of food to the table. Light music in the background. Toasts and jokes. Shoes optional.

. . .

The Menus

AL FRESCO DREAM

Aperitivo: Grissini (page 103) with prosciutto

Bevande: Spritz Aperol (page 135)

Antipasto: Fiori di Zucca (page 92)

Primo: Spaghetti al Pomodoro (page 108) with fresh basil

Secondo: Polpette (page 124)

Contorno: Verdure al Forno (page 100)

Dolce: Pesche Caramellate (page 132) with a scoop of vanilla gelato

LIGHT, BREEZY, FROM THE SEA

Aperitivo: Chilled white wine and summer Bruschetta (page 40)

Antipasto: Polpo e Patate (page 88)

Primo: Spaghetti alla Vongole (page 112)

Dolce: Torta al Limone e Olio d'Oliva (page 131) with powdered sugar

Bevande: Limoncello Fatto in Casa (page 136) served in chilled glasses

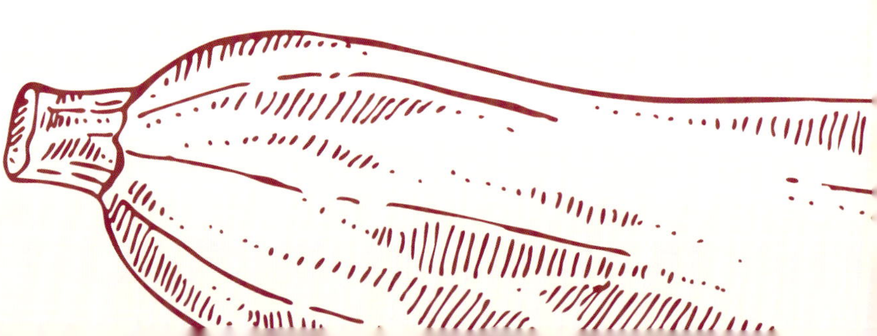

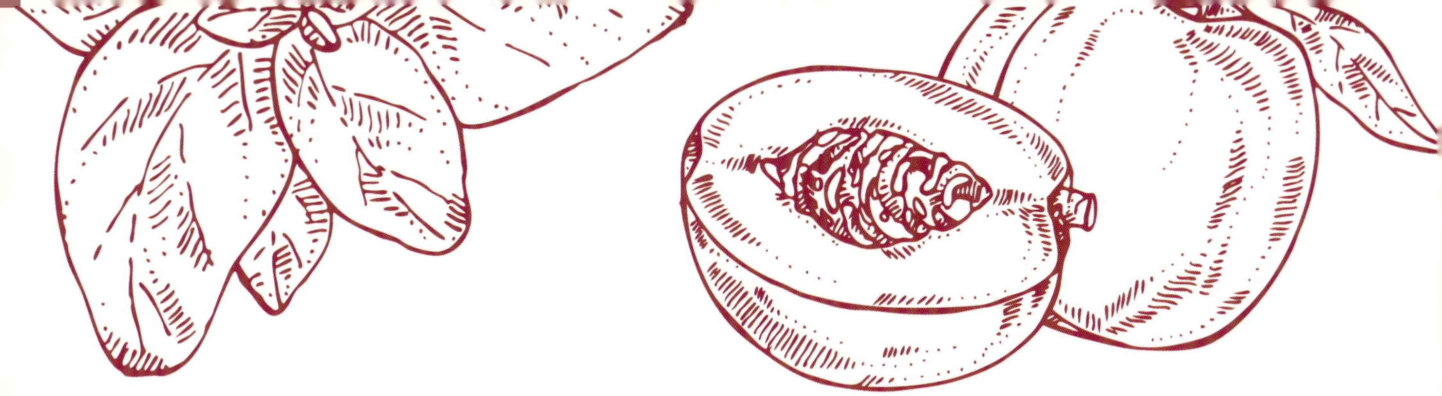

Set the Scene

- Set the table ahead of time—cloth napkins, small flower or herb jars, a mix of votive and taper candles.
- Prepare a big pitcher of Spritz Aperol or a fun mocktail ahead of time to set the tone.

. . .

Welcome Your Guests

- Don't send guests to the fridge. Instead, have drinks and water chilling in a bucket, a cooler, or a pretty pitcher on the table.
- Put food on the table before they ask. Hospitality means anticipating, not reacting. Even if it's just Grissini and olives—something must be out when they arrive. It'll break the ice and rev up the appetite.
- Encourage your guests to help with the food prep. Make it an immersive experience, almost like a cooking class.

. . .

Savor the Meal

- Keep it light and fresh—it's not essential to have antipasto, primo, and secondo, especially in the summer. Remember, it's hot and no one wants to be overly stuffed.
- Consider making just one showstopper (something like a whole platter of Pesche Caramellate or Fiori di Zucca). It will be a conversation starter.
- Don't apologize if you're "just" serving pasta. You're not hosting a banquet. You're hosting a vibe. A big bowl of perfectly made pasta is the main event.
- Send guests home full, happy, and with leftovers. Because the only thing better than dinner with friends … is a slice of lemon cake for breakfast the next morning.

Autunno

Fall

antipasti e contorni

Frittelle di Cavolfiore

Fried Cauliflower Fritters

. . .

4 servings

These crispy fritters are what we make when we want a cozy snack or an easy-but-delicious side to accompany a hearty main dish. They're golden on the outside, soft on the inside, and tempting enough to eat straight from the pan. The ingredients are simple, but once you mix them up and fry them, you've got a plate of cauliflower that the kids will actually fight over.

Don't worry about forming them into perfect rounds. They're meant to look rustic and should be easy. You can finish them with a sprinkle of freshly cracked black pepper or, our personal favorite, some more grated Parmigiano Reggiano. Warning: Don't expect any leftovers!

1 lb (454 g) cauliflower
2 oz (57 g) freshly grated Parmigiano Reggiano
Sea salt and pepper, to taste
2 large eggs, lightly beaten
¾ cup (90 g) all-purpose flour
1 to 2 tbsp extra virgin olive oil

Special Equipment

Potato masher (optional)

1 Wash the cauliflower and cut it into even 1-inch (2.5 cm) florets.

2 Add ¼ inch (6 mm) of water to a large sauté pan, add the florets, and cover. Bring to a simmer over medium heat and steam for 5 to 7 minutes. The cauliflower should be fork tender but not mushy. Drain the excess water.

3 Place the steamed cauliflower into a large bowl and mash it with a potato masher or fork until smooth, with only a few small lumps remaining.

4 Add the Parmigiano Reggiano, salt, and pepper. Stir to combine.

5 Add the eggs and flour, mixing with a spoon or your hands to fully combine. It should create a lumpy mixture.

6 Add the olive oil to the same pan over medium-low heat.

7 Drop large spoonfuls of the cauliflower mixture into the pan, flatten them into ½-inch (1.25 cm) patties with a spatula, and cook for 3 to 4 minutes per side, until golden. Cook the fritters in batches so you don't overcrowd the pan. Meanwhile, preheat the oven to 400°F (200°C).

8 Allow the fritters to rest on a paper towel–lined plate as you finish frying the rest of the mixture.

9 After you finish, arrange the fritters in a single layer on a parchment-lined baking sheet and bake for 8 to 12 minutes, until the middles are cooked through and the edges are crisp.

antipasti e contorni

Spinaci ai Formaggi

Cheesy Spinach

. . .

4 servings

This cheesy spinach is one of those humble little side dishes that ends up stealing the show. It's creamy and buttery, and a touch of nutmeg is enough to make it feel fancy.

The first time I had it, Alessio's mom made it for us, and it rekindled my love of spinach. I'm not kidding. I looked over at Alessio mid-bite, and he swore that he'd learn to make it for me, and he did. It's now one of our favorite cozy sides, whether we're pairing it with breaded chicken cutlets or grilled meat or just spooning it onto our plates like it's the main event. If you've never had spinach like this, get ready. You'll never go back to the plain sautéed version again.

4 lbs (1.8 kg) fresh spinach
Extra virgin olive oil
3 tbsp unsalted butter
1 white onion, diced
1 garlic clove, minced
Pinch of ground nutmeg
Sea salt and pepper, to taste
3½ oz (100 g) freshly grated mozzarella (grated with the largest holes of a box grater)
3½ oz (100 g) finely grated Parmigiano Reggiano

1. Add the spinach to a large sauté pan over medium-low heat, drizzle it with olive oil, and cook until wilted, 2 to 3 minutes.
2. Once cooked, drain the spinach and allow to cool slightly before using your hands or a towel to squeeze out all of the excess water. Set aside to cool completely before chopping it into small pieces.
3. Melt the butter in the same pan over medium-low heat, add the onion, and cook for 5 to 7 minutes, until softened and golden.
4. Add the spinach, garlic, nutmeg, salt, and pepper to the pan and cook for 1 to 2 minutes, until fragrant.
5. Add both cheeses. Reduce the heat to low and stir until melted and well combined. You can add a splash of water, if needed, to make everything smooth and creamy.

Polenta e Funghi

Polenta and Mushrooms

. . .

4 servings

There's a saying in Friuli, Alessio's home region in Northern Italy, that goes "Al è miei polenta cencia nuja, che nuja cencia polenta." It means "It's better to have polenta without anything, than nothing without polenta." In other words, polenta is the kind of food that makes a meal all on its own, and you should always be grateful for it, even if you have something simple on the table.

This dish is one of Alessio's comfort meals, and it's one of the first things he took me to try when we visited his hometown for the first time. It's what tastes like "home" for him. The polenta is simple and soft and the mushrooms are sautéed in garlic, parsley, and wine until silky, and when combined, they become one of those perfect fall meals. The kind that makes you want another scoop even if you're full.

Polenta doesn't always get the love it deserves in the US. To be honest, it took me a while to develop a taste for it, but now I love it! We think it's time to change polenta's reputation from boring to comforting, earthy, and timeless. We didn't include this in the recipe below, but if you want your polenta to be extra comforting, stir in 1 to 2 tablespoons of butter at the end of cooking before turning it out onto a plate. You can also finish with a sprinkle of Parmigiano Reggiano.

For the polenta (see Note):

8 cups (2 L) water

1 tsp sea salt

4 cups (500 g) coarse or medium ground cornmeal

For the mushrooms (see Note):

7 oz (200 g) champignon mushrooms

5 oz (142 g) oyster mushrooms

5 oz (142 g) fresh porcini mushrooms

1 tbsp extra virgin olive oil

1 garlic clove, peeled and crushed

½ cup (120 ml) white wine

½ cup (120 ml) vegetable broth

1 tbsp unsalted butter

Handful of fresh parsley, roughly chopped

1. *To make the polenta:* Bring the water to a boil in a deep stock pot over high heat. Salt the water once it's boiling.
2. Add in the cornmeal, little by little, while stirring constantly.
3. Bring the mixture back to a boil, constantly stirring to prevent burning or clumping.
4. Reduce the heat to low. Continue to cook for 60 minutes, stirring constantly to prevent burning, until the polenta is thick, creamy, and pulling away from the sides of the pot when stirring.
5. Once finished, turn the polenta out onto a large plate. Cover the polenta with a kitchen towel to keep warm while preparing the mushrooms, if desired.
6. *To make the mushrooms:* Clean the mushrooms and cut them into halves or quarters, depending on the size. Be sure to keep the types of mushrooms separated even after chopping.
7. Add the olive oil and garlic to a large sauté pan over medium heat and cook for 1 to 2 minutes, until fragrant.
8. Add in the oyster and porcini mushrooms and cook for 5 to 7 minutes.
9. Reduce the heat to low and add the white wine. Continue cooking, uncovered, until the alcohol has evaporated and the mushrooms are soft, 15 to 20 minutes. About 10 minutes from the end of cooking, add in the champignon mushrooms, broth, and butter to help finish the cooking.

10 Once the mushrooms are fully cooked and soft, remove from the heat and stir in the parsley.

11 Serve the mushrooms hot over the cooked polenta.

NOTE

You can also use instant polenta instead of the traditional method, as it's quite time-consuming to constantly stir for 1 hour straight. If using instant, simply follow the cooking instructions on the package and begin with preparing the mushrooms. Also, different mushrooms are available in different areas. If you can't find the varieties mentioned in the ingredient list, feel free to substitute with your favorite kinds.

antipasti e contorni

Crocchette di Patate

Potato Croquettes

. . .

4 servings

These are so good that it's kind of ridiculous. Crispy on the outside, soft and pillowy on the inside. In Alessio's childhood home, they were a staple alongside roast chicken, but honestly, they go with just about everything. Word of advice? Make more than you think you need. You think you'll eat just a few but then suddenly, the platter is empty. They're the kind of dish that's simple, crowd-pleasing, and impossible to stop eating once you start.

2 lbs (907 g) yellow potatoes
2 large egg yolks
2½ oz (70 g) grated Parmigiano Reggiano
2 tbsp all-purpose flour
Pinch of ground nutmeg
Sea salt and pepper, to taste
2 large eggs, for breading
1 cup (120 g) plain dry breadcrumbs
Preferred oil, for frying

Special Equipment
Potato masher or ricer
Candy or deep-fry thermometer

1. Wash and scrub the potatoes and then place them whole into a large pot and cover them with water. Bring to a boil over high heat and allow them to cook until soft when pricked with a fork or knife, 20 to 30 minutes.
2. When the potatoes are soft, rinse them under cold water to help release and remove the peel. Place the potatoes into a large bowl.
3. Use a potato masher or ricer to create fluffy, lightly mashed potatoes.
4. Add the egg yolks, Parmigiano Reggiano, flour, nutmeg, salt, and pepper to the potatoes and stir to combine.
5. Form the croquettes. Using your hands, take about ¼ cup of the mixture and roll it into a log about 3 inches (7.5 cm) long by 1 inch (2.5 cm) wide. Slightly flatten each end to create a cylinder shape. Place it on a parchment-lined baking sheet and repeat until you have 25 to 30 croquettes. If you feel that the croquettes are too soft, you can chill them in the fridge for 20 to 30 minutes before moving to the next step.
6. Whisk the eggs in a bowl and spread the breadcrumbs out on a flat surface like a plate.
7. One by one, dip each croquette into the egg mixture, gently tapping off the excess, and then roll in the breadcrumbs to coat. Set aside on the parchment paper.
8. When the croquettes are ready, heat the oil in a large deep pot to 350°F (180°C). Fry the croquettes in four batches until deep golden brown on all sides, 3 to 4 minutes. Be careful not to overcrowd the pot.
9. Allow to drain on a paper towel-lined plate until finished. Serve immediately.

antipasti e contorni

Castagne al Forno

Oven-Roasted Chestnuts

. . .

4 to 6 servings

There's something unmistakably autumnal about the smell of chestnuts roasting. It fills the air with warmth and makes you want to snuggle up around a fire and slow down for a while. In Italy, chestnuts are a staple of the colder months. You'll often find them sold at street markets in large paper cones. The centers are soft, nutty, and surprisingly sweet. They also have a somewhat crumbly texture that's a cross between a baked potato and a roasted almond.

We wanted to recreate that delicious snack at home, so we began roasting chestnuts in the oven. We were pleasantly surprised that they were just as good as the ones we have at the Monday market near Alessio's hometown.

2 lbs (907 g) chestnuts

1. Take each chestnut and use a sharp knife to slice an x across the front of each.
2. Fill a large bowl with water and soak the chestnuts for 2 hours.
3. Preheat the oven to 350°F (180°C). Drain the chestnuts well and pat them dry.
4. Spread the chestnuts evenly on a parchment-lined baking sheet and bake for 25 to 30 minutes.
5. Once finished, allow to rest for 15 minutes before peeling and enjoying!

antipasti e contorni

Pane di Segale

Rye Sourdough Bread

. . .

1 loaf

The rhythmic process of making bread has always been comforting to me. It takes time and patience, but the reward is a rustic, flavorful loaf and a kitchen filled with the heavenly aroma of fresh bread. This rye sourdough feels like it came right out of a wood-burning stove in some quaint alpine village.

Rye bread is common in Northern Italy, especially in colder regions where you want something hearty and nourishing. A touch of molasses gives it a subtle sweetness, but it still pairs perfectly with savory cheese or soups like Vellutata di Zucca e Carota (Pumpkin Carrot Soup, page 155).

This isn't a throw-it-together kind of bread. It forces you to slow down and go through the process, but the result is a loaf that feels homey and rustic and will make you want to turn around and make another one the next day.

1½ cups (360 ml) warm water
3½ oz (100 g) sourdough starter
2 tsp (12 g) molasses
2 tsp (12 g) honey
2 cups (250 g) bread flour
1⅔ cups (200 g) dark rye flour
2 tsp (10 g) sea salt
Rice flour, for shaping

Special Equipment
Wooden spoon
Banneton (optional)
Dutch oven

1 Combine the water, sourdough starter, molasses, and honey in a large bowl.

2 Add the bread flour, rye flour, and salt, and mix with a wooden spoon until combined.

3 Cover the bowl with a damp kitchen towel and place in a warm spot to rise for 1 hour.

4 Stretch and fold the dough inside the bowl by gently lifting up an edge of the dough and pulling it up to stretch it a bit before folding it to the center. Continue around the entire dough ball, and you will have completed a "stretch and fold." Do two or three rounds of this before covering with the damp towel and placing in a warm spot for 30 minutes.

5 Every 30 minutes, for 2½ hours, complete another full round of stretch and folds. This should give you an additional five rounds.

6 Cover again with the towel and allow to bulk ferment until the dough is almost doubled in size, roughly 4 hours at 70 to 72°F (21.1 to 22.2°C). The timing for this will vary based on the temperature of your environment; it will take longer in colder homes than in warmer ones.

7 Once bulk fermentation is complete, lightly flour a hard surface with rice flour.

8 Turn out the dough so it is upside down on the counter (smooth side down, sticky/rough side up).

9 Shape the dough into a boule (round loaf) by lifting the edges and folding to the center like you did during the stretch and folds. Make sure the top surface of the dough is tight with tension.

NOTE

Store the bread wrapped in paper or wrapped loosely in a clean kitchen towel and placed in a bread box. It should keep fresh for about 2 days. If you want to store for longer, slice the bread and place inside a sealed freezer bag or container and freeze.

10 Place the dough smooth side down into a floured banneton or a bowl lined with a floured kitchen towel. Cover with a very damp towel and place in the fridge to rise overnight.

11 When you are ready to bake, preheat the oven to 475°F (245°C) with a Dutch oven inside.

12 When the oven is preheated, take the dough straight from the fridge and gently flip it onto a piece of parchment paper, with the smooth side up. Score the dough by using a sharp knife or bread lame to cut a slightly curved line from one end to the other, making sure to slice at a 45° angle.

13 Lower the oven temperature to 450°F (230°C), place the dough on the parchment paper inside the Dutch oven, carefully close the lid, and put in the oven to bake for 20 minutes.

14 Remove the lid, lower the oven temperature to 430°F (220°C), and bake for an additional 20 to 25 minutes, until the crust is brown and crisp.

15 Remove and place on a cooling rack for at least 2 hours before slicing. Do not slice earlier, or the inside of the bread will be gummy. (See Note.)

piatti principali

Vellutata di Zucca e Carota

Pumpkin Carrot Soup

. . .

4 servings

This soup came together one chilly evening when Alessio decided he wanted to make something super autumnal. Something with pumpkin in it! He created a simple recipe, and every time he made it, he tweaked it a little bit more until it became the version you see below, which we now eat multiple times every single fall.

The potatoes give it a hearty texture, while the sweetness of the pumpkin and carrots blends beautifully with the savory cheese that we spoon on top. Pair it with toasted bread or crackers and you have the perfect meal when there's a chill in the air.

- 1 tbsp extra virgin olive oil, plus more for serving
- ¼ yellow onion, diced
- 1 medium pie pumpkin, peeled, seeded, and cut into 1-inch (2.5 cm) cubes
- 3 medium carrots, chopped
- 4 small Yukon gold potatoes, cut into 1-inch (2.5 cm) cubes
- 4 to 5 cups (1 to 1¼ L) water or vegetable broth
- Sea salt, to taste
- Grated Parmigiano Reggiano, for serving
- Toasted bread or crackers, for serving

Special Equipment

Blender or immersion blender

1. Warm the olive oil in a medium stockpot over low heat. Add the onion and cook for 5 to 7 minutes, until softened and golden. Be careful not to burn.
2. Add the pumpkin, carrots, and potatoes to the pot. Pour in enough water or broth to just cover the vegetables. Stir.
3. Increase the heat to high, bring the mixture to a boil, and then add the salt.
4. Reduce the heat to low and simmer for 30 to 35 minutes, until the pumpkin is fully softened. Check the doneness by pressing the pumpkin with the back of a spoon or fork. It should smash easily. Remove from the heat.
5. Blend the soup until smooth and creamy.
6. Ladle the soup into bowls and finish with a drizzle of olive oil and a generous amount of grated Parmigiano Reggiano. Serve alongside toasted bread or crackers.

piatti principali

Vellutata di Porro

Leek Soup

. . .

4 servings

This is one of those classic soups that stands the test of time. It's gentle and creamy, but also quietly elegant. It's comforting, without being too heavy.

Leeks and potatoes are a timeless pairing across much of Europe, and this version leans into their natural, soft texture. There's no butter or cream, just simple ingredients and good olive oil. It's perfect on a cold night with freshly made bread—try our Pane di Segale (Rye Sourdough Bread, page 152)—and candlelight.

4 or 5 leeks

1 to 2 tbsp extra virgin olive oil, plus more for serving

Sea salt, to taste

2 lbs (907 g) yellow potatoes

9 cups (2.2 L) water

Black pepper (optional)

Special Equipment

Immersion blender

1. Clean the leeks thoroughly, taking care to wash away any dirt and debris, and slice the white and light green parts into thin rounds. Rinse again to make sure they are clean.
2. Warm the olive oil in a medium stockpot over medium-low heat. Add the sliced leeks and salt and cook for 7 to 8 minutes to soften.
3. Meanwhile, peel the potatoes and cut them into ½-inch (1.25 cm) cubes.
4. Add the potatoes and enough water to cover the vegetables. Cook for 25 minutes, stirring occasionally, or until the potatoes are softened. Test the potatoes with a fork or knife to make sure they are soft.
5. Remove the pot from the heat and use an immersion blender to blend the soup until the vegetables are pureed and you have a smooth and creamy texture.
6. Season with more salt, to taste.
7. Divide the soup into bowls, drizzle with olive oil, and season with pepper, if desired.

piatti principali

Minestrone

Hearty Vegetable Soup

. . .

4 to 6 servings

The first time Alessio's mom told me she was going to make minestrone, I was expecting the thin tomato-based soup with a few beans and pasta that I've seen so often at Italian restaurants in the US. What I got instead completely changed the way I thought about this dish.

Her version had everything: chickpeas, cannellini beans, farro, zucchini, carrots, kale, chard, cabbage, etc. Anything she had on hand made it into the pot. It was hearty, nourishing, and flavorful. Every bite tasted like she'd been making it forever, even though it's not quite the same soup twice. I fell in love instantly. I could've eaten ten bowls. Now, every time we go to visit, I shamelessly ask her to make it for me, whether it's cold outside or the middle of summer. It's just that good.

- ½ cup (90 g) dry cannellini beans (see Note)
- ½ cup (90 g) dry chickpeas (garbanzo beans) (see Note)
- 4 handfuls farro (about ½ cup/70 g)
- 1 tbsp extra virgin olive oil
- ½ red onion, diced
- 1 garlic clove, minced
- 2 medium carrots, diced
- 2 medium zucchinis, diced
- 1 celery stalk, diced
- ½ leek, washed and thinly sliced
- 1 lb (454 g) yellow potatoes, diced
- 2 cups (140 g) thinly sliced Savoy cabbage
- 3 cups (90 g) chopped baby spinach leaves
- 1 cup (100 g) Italian-style flat green beans, cut into thirds
- Handful of Swiss chard leaves, chopped
- Handful of Tuscan kale, chopped
- 4 to 6 cups (1 to 1.4 L) vegetable broth
- ½ cup (120 ml) water, plus more as needed
- 3 fresh sage leaves, chopped
- 2 sprigs fresh rosemary, stems removed and leaves chopped
- Salt and pepper, to taste
- Crusty bread of choice, for serving

Special Equipment

Immersion blender

1. Soak the cannellini beans and chickpeas in water overnight.
2. Drain and rinse the soaked beans and chickpeas before adding them to a medium saucepan and covering them with water. Cook uncovered for about 1 hour, or until soft. Drain and set aside.
3. Cook the farro in a medium pot of water according to the package instructions (typically 20 to 40 minutes, depending on the type of farro).
4. Warm the olive oil in a large pot over low heat. Add the onion and cook for 5 to 7 minutes, until softened and golden.
5. Add the garlic and cook for 1 minute, until fragrant.
6. Add in the carrots, zucchini, celery, leek, potatoes, and cabbage. Cook for about 10 minutes, or until the vegetables soften. Add a bit of water if needed.
7. Add the spinach, green beans, chard, and kale to the pot of vegetables. Deglaze with some of the broth.
8. Place half of the cooked bean mixture in a separate bowl and, using an immersion blender, blend it into a creamy consistency with about ½ cup (120 ml) of water.

NOTE

Canned beans are a suitable substitute. $1\frac{1}{2}$ cups (390 g) of each should do the trick. Just be sure to drain and wash the beans first.

9 Add the remaining broth, the creamy bean mixture, the remaining whole beans, and the farro to the pot of cooked vegetables. Add the sage, rosemary, salt, and pepper. Add enough water to bring up the liquid amount so that it covers all of the vegetables.

10 Cook on low for 30 to 40 minutes, stirring occasionally.

11 Serve warm with crusty bread.

piatti principali

Pasta e Fagioli

Pasta and Beans

...

2 servings

This might be one of my all-time favorite Italian dishes, and honestly, I can't explain why. It doesn't look like much, but there's something about the soft beans mixed with the chew of the pasta that hits at my love for comfort food. It's creamy without cream, rich without meat, and deeply satisfying when you need something cozy.

Once, in the middle of July, I asked for Pasta e Fagioli at a restaurant in Italy, and the waiter looked at me like I'd just asked him for a cup of hot chocolate at the beach. "I'm sorry, miss," he said. "We don't have the ingredients for that. It's a fall dish." I was heartbroken ... but also, I kind of loved that response. It was so Italian. In Italy, food isn't just about a craving. It's rhythm, and season, and waiting a whole year for your beloved dish to come back again. Pasta e Fagioli belongs to the colder months. (Don't tell that waiter, but I'm still making it in July.)

1½ cups (270 g) dry borlotti beans (or cranberry beans; see Note)
2 or 3 sage leaves
1 sprig of rosemary
1 garlic clove, peeled and crushed
1 tbsp extra virgin olive oil
1 large carrot, diced
1 celery, diced
½ yellow onion, diced
1 tbsp tomato paste
3½ oz (100 g) dry short pasta (elbow, lumache, ditalini, shells, etc.)
1 to 2 cups (240 to 480 ml) vegetable broth
Sea salt and pepper, to taste

Special Equipment

Butcher's twine
Blender or immersion blender

1. Soak the beans overnight in a medium bowl of water.
2. Use the butcher's twine to tie together the sage leaves and rosemary into a little herb bundle.
3. Drain and rinse the beans before cooking them and the garlic in a large pot of salted water over medium-high heat for 1 hour.
4. Move half of the cooked beans and the garlic to a separate medium bowl and use a blender or immersion blender to blend them with a bit of water to create a creamy mixture.
5. Drain the remaining whole beans and set them aside.
6. Warm the olive oil in a large stockpot over medium-low heat.
7. Add the carrot, celery, and onion and cook for 7 to 8 minutes, until the vegetables are softened. Make sure not to burn them.
8. Add the whole beans and tomato paste and stir to combine.
9. Add the blended beans, herb bundle, and pasta. Put just enough broth into the pot to cover. Add salt and pepper to taste.
10. Reduce the heat to low and cook uncovered for the time indicated on the pasta packaging. Continue adding broth as needed while the pasta cooks. The broth will evaporate, so you want to maintain enough liquid to continue cooking the pasta, without making the dish too watery.
11. Once the pasta is fully cooked, remove and discard the herb bundle before serving.

NOTE

Borlotti beans are traditional, but we've also used cannellini or kidney beans, and the dish turns out great!

piatti principali

Risotto Salsiccia e Radicchio

Sausage and Radicchio Risotto

. . .

4 servings

This dish is a classic in Alessio's circle of friends and family. The first time I had it, I was immediately hooked. There's something about the slight bitterness of radicchio that mixes perfectly with the richness of the sausage and makes for the perfect combination. After that, I started to ask for sausage and radicchio on my pasta, on my pizza, you name it. But risotto is where this combo truly shines.

One important note if you're making this recipe in the US: We've noticed that most "Italian sausage" here is loaded with fennel. And while that might work in some dishes, it will completely throw off the flavor of this dish. The sausage we use in Italy is simple, so read the label or talk to your butcher and try to find something as plain as possible and without fennel. Also, if you can find it, look for radicchio di Treviso. It's a variety that's traditionally used in this dish. It's longer, thinner, and less bitter than the rounder version of radicchio that you usually see in US grocery stores. However, it's tricky to find, so we use the traditional radicchio, too.

- 7 oz (200 g) red radicchio
- 5½ tbsp unsalted butter, divided
- 1 small red onion, diced
- 2 tbsp extra virgin olive oil
- 1½ cups (300 g) dry arborio rice
- 1 cup (240 ml) red wine, divided
- 6⅓ cups (1.5 L) vegetable broth
- 7 oz (200 g) sausage
- 2 oz (57 g) freshly grated Parmigiano Reggiano
- Sea salt and pepper, to taste

1. Wash and finely chop the radicchio.
2. Melt half of the butter in a large sauté pan over medium-low heat. Add the onion and olive oil, and cook for 5 to 7 minutes, until softened and golden.
3. Add the radicchio and cook for 4 to 5 minutes.
4. Add the rice and stir to toast for 3 minutes.
5. Add in half of the red wine and allow the alcohol to evaporate.
6. Heat the broth in a medium saucepan over medium heat. Cover and keep warm.
7. Cook the rice by adding the hot broth a little at a time. Start with a few ladles, adding more as the mixture dries out. Never allow it to dry out completely.
8. Remove the sausage from its casing (if needed) and roughly chop.
9. Add the sausage to a separate medium pan over medium-low heat and cook for 5 to 7 minutes, until browned. Drain the grease from the pan, pour in the remaining wine, and continue to cook the sausage while allowing the alcohol to evaporate, 4 to 5 minutes.
10. Add the sausage to the pan of rice to finish cooking.
11. Once the sausage and rice are fully cooked (typically 15 to 18 minutes for the rice), remove from the heat and stir in the remaining butter and the Parmigiano Reggiano, salt, and pepper. Stir well until creamy and combined.

piatti principali

Risotto alla Milanese

Milan-Style Risotto

. . .

4 servings

This is one of the most iconic dishes in Northern Italy. Possibly the most elegant risotto of them all! Risotto alla Milanese has deep roots in the Lombardy region and is known for its striking gold color. That color actually comes from saffron, one of the most prized (and priciest) spices in the world.

Traditionally, this dish is served with Ossobuco (page 180), but it's also delicious on its own. It's rich, buttery, savory, and wonderfully aromatic because of the saffron. And then there's the bone marrow … the traditional ingredient that gives the dish its unmistakable silky finish. Bone marrow can be difficult to find, especially in the US. If your butcher has marrow bones, you can simmer them down and scoop out the marrow before cooking. If not, you can skip it and still have a wonderful risotto. It just technically won't be "alla Milanese." (But don't worry, your secret is safe with us.)

1 tsp saffron threads
½ cup (120 ml) warm water
7 tbsp unsalted butter, divided
½ medium yellow onion, finely diced
4 cups (1 L) beef broth, divided
1 tbsp bone marrow
1¾ cups (350 g) dry carnaroli rice
Sea salt, to taste
2 oz (57 g) freshly grated Parmigiano Reggiano

1. Put the saffron threads in a small bowl. Take a few spoonfuls of warm water (about ½ cup/120 ml total) and pour them over the saffron to steep for 30 minutes.
2. Melt 3 tablespoons of butter in a large saucepan over medium-low heat, and then add the onion. Add a spoonful or two of broth into the pan to stew the onions. Cook for 2 to 3 minutes, until slightly softened.
3. Add the bone marrow. (See Note.) When the marrow dissolves, turn off the heat. Set the pan off to the side.
4. In a medium saucepan, heat the remaining beef broth on high and bring to a boil. Then lower to medium heat and maintain a simmer.
5. In a large sauté pan over low heat, add 2 tablespoons of butter, allow it to melt, and then add the rice. Toast for 2 to 3 minutes, until translucent. Add ladles of the hot beef broth, a few at a time, to begin cooking the rice. The broth should always just cover the top of the rice. Stir continuously. As the rice absorbs the broth, add more to continue cooking.
6. After 10 minutes, add the onion and marrow mixture to the rice.
7. After 4 to 6 minutes more (about 2 minutes before the end of cooking), add the bloomed saffron and its liquid.
8. When the rice is almost done (it should take about 16 to 18 minutes total to cook), add salt to taste.
9. Remove the pot from the heat and add the remaining 2 tablespoons of butter and the Parmigiano Reggiano and stir until creamy.

NOTE

It is not very easy to find beef bone marrow; however, you can ask your butcher for a couple of beef marrow bones cut in half. While warming the beef broth, add the bones to the stock and let them boil for a few minutes. Remove and let cool slightly. You should then be able to scoop out the bone marrow with a spoon.

piatti principali

Frico Friulano

Friulian Cheese and Potato Crisp

. . .

2 to 4 servings

This is a dish that says "Friuli" louder than anything else on the table. Because it's his home region, Alessio is incredibly proud of it. And honestly, he should be proud, because frico is ridiculously good. Golden and crispy on the outside, soft and cheesy on the inside, it's the ultimate comfort food.

In fact, frico gets its own celebration in a small village near Alessio's home. Every year on August 10th, there's a local festival where the star of the show is frico served with heaps of polenta and the best french fries you've ever put in your mouth.

Traditional frico is made with two ages of Montasio cheese (a young and an old), but since that type of cheese can be hard to find outside of Italy, this version uses Gruyère and Piave. They are perfect substitutes that will give the same gooey, crunchy magic. However, if you happen to get lucky and stumble across some Montasio, scoop it up and get a taste of the authentic frico. It's rich, rustic, and addictive.

3 large yellow potatoes
2 tbsp unsalted butter
1 white onion, thinly sliced
7 oz (200 g) Gruyère, cubed
7 oz (200 g) Piave, cubed

Special Equipment
10-inch (25 cm) skillet
Two wooden spoons

1. Peel the potatoes and grate them with the large holes on a box grater.
2. Melt the butter in a 10-inch (25 cm) skillet with low edges over low heat.
3. Add the onion and potatoes to the pan. Use two wooden spoons to mix gently (scooping from the outside in), taking care not to let the onion burn. Cook until the onion softens and the potatoes become tender, 10 to 12 minutes.
4. Add the Gruyère and Piave to the mixture. With two wooden spoons, continue to mix and stir until the cheeses melt and the ingredients are well combined, 7 to 10 minutes.
5. Using the wooden spoons, shape the mixture into a shallow circle the width of the pan. Allow it to form a crispy crust, 10 to 12 minutes. Check it by gently lifting the edge, but try not to lift the frico too much, as it needs to cook undisturbed to form a crust.
6. Once the crust is formed, the frico should release from the pan when gently shaken. Carefully flip it to create a crust on the other side.
7. Slide the frico out onto a plate and slice it into wedges. It is traditionally served with a side of polenta.

Gnocchi di Zucca

Pumpkin Gnocchi

. . .

2 servings

This dish tastes like fall. Soft, golden gnocchi are tossed in a butter and sage sauce, ready to be gobbled down on a chilly evening. It's one of the most beloved cold-weather meals in Northern Italy.

Traditionally, these gnocchi are made with zucca di Mantova (Mantua pumpkin), a sweet, flavorful pumpkin with low moisture and a velvety texture. If you can find one, it's absolutely worth using. However, we've made delicious gnocchi with pie pumpkins and even butternut squash. Just keep in mind that different pumpkins have different amounts of moisture. That means your dough might need more or less flour to come together. Trust your hands to know. The dough should be soft but workable, not sticky or overly dense.

For the gnocchi:

14 oz (400 g) pumpkin (Mantua preferred, but you can sub with pie pumpkin or even butternut squash) (see Note)

Extra virgin olive oil

Sea salt

1 sprig rosemary

1 large egg

⅔ cup (80 g) all-purpose flour, plus more as needed

Pinch of ground nutmeg

For the sauce:

4 tbsp unsalted butter

Fresh sage, to taste (about 4 or 5 leaves)

Grated Parmigiano Reggiano (optional)

Special Equipment

Basting brush (optional)

Potato ricer

NOTE

Pumpkin puree made from fresh pumpkin is best, as the canned pumpkin puree has too much moisture.

1. *To make the gnocchi:* Preheat the oven to 350°F (180°C). Line a baking sheet with parchment paper.
2. Slice the pumpkin into 1-to-2-inch (2.5 to 5 cm) slices and place them on the prepared baking sheet.
3. Drizzle with olive oil, sprinkle with salt, and hand tear the rosemary leaves on top of the slices. Use a basting brush or your hands to fully coat both sides.
4. Bake for about 30 minutes and then allow the pumpkin slices to cool until you can handle them.
5. Remove the peel and pass the pumpkin slices through a ricer into a large bowl.
6. Add the egg, the flour, a pinch of salt, and the nutmeg and use your hands to knead everything into a slightly firm but moldable dough. Depending on the type of pumpkin you use, you might need to add more flour to get the right consistency, as some pumpkin varieties have more moisture than others.
7. Divide the dough into quarters on a lightly floured surface and roll each out into a long log about ¾ inch (2 cm) thick.
8. Cut the logs into 1 inch (2.5 cm) long pieces, quickly rolling each piece in flour to prevent sticking.
9. You can either press each piece along the back end of a pronged fork to achieve the classic ridges or leave them smooth.
10. Once all the gnocchi are ready, bring a pot of salted water to a boil. Add the gnocchi and cook until they float to the surface, 2 to 3 minutes.
11. *To make the sauce:* Melt the butter in a large saucepan over low heat and add the sage leaves, cooking for 1 to 2 minutes, until fragrant. Add the gnocchi to the pan and toss gently to coat. Serve immediately, topping with grated Parmigiano Reggiano if desired.

piatti principali

Pizzoccheri

Buckwheat Cabbage Pasta from Valtellina

. . .

4 servings

We first tried this dish in Tirano, a small alpine town in Northern Italy, just before boarding the Bernina Express. We ordered it because we'd heard it was traditional, but we had no idea what we were in for. When the plate arrived, we saw brown bits of pasta, cabbage, potatoes, cheese, and butter. All delicious ingredients on their own, but together? We were about to find out. One bite and we looked at each other and knew we were eating something special. We wanted to order another serving immediately.

Pizzoccheri comes from the Valtellina region of Lombardy, the kind of cold, mountainous place where people need food that will keep them full and warm them up. Like many Italian dishes originating in the mountain regions, it features modest ingredients, earthy flavors, buttery richness, and delicious melted cheese. It's a true cucina povera or "poor kitchen" dish, but it feels like luxury when you eat it. It is traditionally made with Valtellina Casera DOP cheese, which comes from the same area. However, we used a substitute of fontina to give the same melty texture, since Valtellina Casera DOP is hard to find outside of the region. You can also substitute in Gruyère or Emmental.

If you've never heard of buckwheat noodles or putting potatoes in your pasta, this recipe might make you hesitate—but trust us. This one will surprise you and keep you coming back for more.

For the pasta:

1⅔ cups (200 g) buckwheat flour

⅓ cup plus 1 tbsp (50 g) all-purpose flour, plus more for the work surface

⅔ cup (160 ml) water

Pinch of sea salt

For the layers:

½ Savoy cabbage, cored and cut into thin strips

2 medium yellow potatoes, peeled and cut into ½-inch (1.25 cm) cubes

8 tbsp unsalted butter

1 garlic clove, minced

6 or 7 fresh sage leaves

8 oz (227 g) fontina, diced

5 oz (142 g) Parmigiano Reggiano, grated

Sea salt and pepper, to taste

Special Equipment

Rolling pin

1. *To make the pasta:* Whisk together the buckwheat flour and all-purpose flour in a large bowl and tip onto a flat work surface. Shape into a mound and make a well in the center.
2. Add the water and salt into the well and, using a fork, slowly incorporate the flour around the edge of the well. Continue mixing in the flour, little by little, until the dough is crumbly.
3. Knead the dough with your hands until it is soft and smooth, but not sticking to your hands. Add a bit more water if it's too dry. Cover the dough in plastic wrap and let it rest for 20 minutes.
4. Lightly flour the work surface and roll out the dough into a rectangle 1/16-inch (1.5 mm) thick.
5. Cut the dough into 3-inch-wide (7.5 cm) strips, dusting each with flour, and stacking them on top of each other. Once they are stacked, cut them again, crosswise, into ⅓-inch (8.5 mm) pieces. You should be left with ⅓ × 3-inch (8.5 × 7.5 cm) pasta noodles. Set them aside to dry while you continue the rest of the dish.
6. *To assemble the layers:* Bring a large pot of salted water to a boil. Add the cabbage and potatoes. Make sure they are fully submerged, and cook for 15 to 20 minutes, or until the potatoes are tender. Drain and set aside.

7 Meanwhile, melt the butter in a small saucepan. Add the garlic and sage, lightly cooking the leaves while browning the butter, 5 to 7 minutes. Set aside.

8 Bring a second pot of salted water to a boil. Add the buckwheat noodles and cook for about 2 to 3 minutes, until they bend easily without breaking and have a soft bite. Drain and set aside.

9 Warm a large sauté pan over low heat. Add one-third of the cabbage and potato mixture, as well as one-third of the noodles, to begin making the first layer. Top with one-third of the Parmigiano Reggiano and fontina. Drizzle a bit of the sage butter on top and add the sage leaves and garlic from the butter saucepan, along with salt and pepper. Continue making the layers until all ingredients are used (roughly three layers).

10 Cover the pan, turn off the heat, and allow the cheese to fully melt, 3 to 5 minutes.

11 Toss everything gently to incorporate, and serve warm.

piatti principali

Pappardelle con Ragù di Lenticchie e Funghi

Pasta with Lentil and Mushroom Sauce

...

4 servings

This is the kind of dish that proves you don't need meat to make a delicious ragù. Lentils and dried mushrooms (we prefer porcini, but shiitake work beautifully, too) come together to create a surprisingly rich, layered, and soulful dish ... the perfect dinner for a cold night in the mountains.

We were drawn to this dish as a way to cut back on meat without feeling like we were missing out on delicious pasta ragù, and trust us, it does the trick. The mushrooms add depth, the lentils add a satisfying bite, and the traditional "soffritto" makes it taste like a recipe that's been passed down through generations.

- 7 oz (200 g) dry brown lentils, rinsed and drained
- 1 tbsp extra virgin olive oil
- ¼ yellow onion, finely chopped
- 1 large carrot, finely chopped
- 1 celery stalk, finely chopped
- 2 sprigs fresh thyme
- 1 garlic clove, minced
- 8 oz (227 g) fresh shiitake mushrooms
- 7 oz (200 g) tomato passata
- ½ cup (120 ml) water
- Sea salt and pepper, to taste
- 8½ oz (240 g) egg papparadelle

1. Check the lentils and remove any that are broken or shriveled. Discard any rocks or other debris.
2. Bring a medium pot of unsalted water to a boil and add the lentils. Cook them uncovered according to the package instructions, typically 40 to 60 minutes, until the lentils are soft but not mushy. Drain when finished.
3. Meanwhile, heat the olive oil in a large sauté pan over medium-low heat. Add the onion and cook for 4 to 5 minutes, until softened.
4. Add the carrot, celery, thyme, and garlic, and cook for 8 to 10 minutes, until the vegetables soften.
5. Add the mushrooms to the pan and sauté for 8 to 10 minutes, until softened.
6. Add the passata and water to the vegetables and stir to combine.
7. Add salt and pepper to taste. Simmer uncovered for about 40 minutes, or until the sauce is thickened and reduced.
8. Add the lentils to the sauce and stir to combine.
9. Meanwhile, bring a large pot of salted water to a boil and cook the pappardelle noodles according to the package instructions.
10. Drain the noodles, add them to the lentil sauce, and stir to combine before serving.

piatti principali

Finocchio, Patate, e Besciamella

Fennel and Potato Bake

. . .

4 servings

Fennel is an extremely popular ingredient in Italy. They shave it raw into a salad or roast it until it's sweet. This recipe takes fennel and turns it into something rich and creamy. In the Southern US, where I grew up, we would probably call this "fennel casserole." The layers of fennel, potatoes, and cheese melt together while baking, and you get that addictive crispy top that only Parmigiano Reggiano can give. You can serve this as a main dish with a salad or as a side dish with roast chicken. Some people don't like fennel because of its licorice-like flavor, but this dish is here to convert you into a fennel lover.

- 2 large fennel bulbs
- 8 medium yellow potatoes
- 1 lb (454 g) mozzarella
- 2¼ cups (511 g) Besciamella (Béchamel Sauce, page 224)
- 3½ oz (100 g) freshly grated Parmigiano Reggiano

1. Preheat the oven to 350°F (180°C).
2. Clean and trim the fennel, and clean and peel the potatoes. Cut everything into very thin slices.
3. Bring a large pot of salted water to a boil, add the fennel, and cook for 5 to 6 minutes. Remove the fennel with a slotted spoon and set aside to cool.
4. Add the potatoes to the same pot and cook for 10 to 12 minutes, until softened. Drain and let cool.
5. Meanwhile, slice the mozzarella into thin rounds.
6. Spread some besciamella in the base of a large baking dish to prevent sticking. Layer one-third of the potato slices over the besciamella. Layer one-third of the fennel slices over the potato slices. Cover generously with about half of the remaining besciamella sauce.
7. Top with one-third of the mozzarella slices and Parmigiano Reggiano.
8. Continue layering until all ingredients are finished and you have three even tiers, ending with a generous layer of Parmigiano Reggiano.
9. Bake uncovered for 30 to 40 minutes. Test for doneness by sliding a knife into the vegetables to check that they are soft and cooked through.
10. Broil on high for 2 to 3 minutes, until the top is golden brown.
11. Let cool for 10 minutes before serving.

piatti principali

Peperoni Ripieni

Stuffed Peppers

. . .

2 servings

Peperoni Ripieni are a beloved staple in Italian home cooking. This is one of those comforting dishes that tastes like home, especially for Alessio, who grew up eating his mom's version of these savory stuffed peppers. They're made with simple ingredients that turn into something gorgeous on the plate, and they're also full of flavor. Baked until bubbly, this dish feels familiar, even if you've never had it before. It's perfect for a Sunday lunch or a cozy evening in. Choose whichever bell peppers are your favorite, but we typically choose a mix of colors because it just looks so pretty.

2 slices sourdough bread
½ cup (120 ml) whole milk
4 bell peppers (red, yellow, or orange)
1 lb (454 g) ground beef
6 oz (170 g) grated provolone (grated with the largest holes of a box grater)
2 oz (57 g) grated Parmigiano Reggiano
2 large eggs, lightly beaten
Chopped fresh parsley, to taste
Sea salt and pepper, to taste
Extra virgin olive oil

1. Preheat the oven to 350°F (180°C).
2. Crumble the bread into a small bowl and add the milk. Set it aside to soak.
3. Wash and dry the peppers. Cut off the tops and remove and discard the seeds and membrane from each pepper. Reserve these pepper bases. For the tops, remove the pepper around the green stem and deseed. Dice the pepper tops finely.
4. Add the ground beef, provolone, Parmigiano Reggiano (reserve a bit for topping at the end), eggs, diced pepper tops, parsley, salt, and pepper to a large bowl. Take the bread from the milk and squeeze it to remove as much milk as possible. Add the bread to the beef mixture.
5. Use your hands to mix until well combined.
6. In a small baking dish, place the peppers cut side up. They should fit snugly together so they don't fall over while cooking.
7. Spoon the mixture into each hollow pepper, pressing down to make sure each pepper is filled.
8. Bake the peppers uncovered for 35 to 40 minutes.
9. Remove from the oven, sprinkle with the reserved Parmigiano Reggiano, and place back into the oven and broil on high for about 3 minutes. Take care not to burn the cheese.
10. Remove from the oven, drizzle with olive oil, and serve.

piatti principali

Spezzatino con Patate

Hearty Beef and Potatoes

. . .

6 servings

This is one of the first dishes I remember eating with Alessio's family. It's iconic in their house. It's also tied to one of my earliest memories of visiting his grandfather, Nonno Dario. He had invited us over for lunch and prepared an unforgettable spread: prosciutto, mortadella, salami, so many different kinds of breads, pickles, pickled vegetables, olives, salad, and more. I was so excited that I ate too much of the antipasto and was full before the main course even arrived. But then Nonno Dario brought out the spezzatino … rich and impossibly tender, it was delicious and paired excellently with the golden potatoes he served it with. I don't think I've ever been more happily full in my life.

Over the years, it's become a signature comfort food in their home. Alessio's mom makes it beautifully, so much so that we filmed her teaching it to our followers and the video became an instant favorite. It's simple, hearty, and filling, the kind of thing someone will suggest if everyone needs a bit of comfort. "Facciamo lo spezzatino?"

- 5 to 7 cups (1.2 to 1.7 L) beef broth
- 2 lbs (907 g) beef chuck (or your preferred cut for stew)
- ¼ cup (30 g) all-purpose flour
- 2 tbsp unsalted butter
- 2 small white onions (about 2½ inches/6.5 cm) across), halved
- 3 large sprigs rosemary
- 2 sprigs thyme
- 4 or 5 fresh sage leaves
- 2 medium carrots, peeled and roughly chopped
- 2 celery stalks, chopped
- Sea salt and pepper, to taste
- 8 to 10 small Yukon gold potatoes
- Fresh radicchio salad, for serving (optional)

1. Warm the broth in a medium pot over medium-low heat.
2. Cut the beef into 2-inch (5 cm) cubes, and roll them lightly in the flour to coat the edges.
3. Melt the butter in a large sauté pan over medium heat and add the beef. Brown the meat, rotating the pieces every so often to get color on all sides, 5 to 10 minutes.
4. Reduce the heat to medium-low and add the onions.
5. Allow the meat to continue browning and cooking, stirring occasionally to prevent sticking or burning, 5 to 10 minutes.
6. Add the rosemary, thyme, and sage. The beef should continue to cook and release its juices, about 10 to 15 minutes.
7. Once the beef is fully cooked, add the carrots, celery, salt, and pepper. You'll know it's cooked when the beef is no longer pink in the center and releases clear juices when pierced with a knife.
8. Add enough warmed beef broth to reach the height of the beef and vegetables, reduce the heat to low, and simmer uncovered for 2 to 3 hours, stirring occasionally. As the liquid evaporates, continue adding more warm broth to prevent the pan from drying out.
9. While the stew cooks, clean and peel the potatoes. Bring a large pot of salted water to a boil, add the potatoes, and boil for 15 to 20 minutes, until tender and easily pierced with a fork or knife.
10. Test the beef for tenderness, make sure the last of the liquid has almost completely evaporated, and season with additional salt, if needed. Remove the rosemary and thyme sprigs and discard.
11. Serve the spezzatino with the boiled potatoes and a fresh radicchio salad, if desired.

Ossobuco

• • •

4 servings

Ossobuco is one of the most beloved dishes in Northern Italy. Slow-braised veal shanks in a savory sauce? It's melt-in-your-mouth good. Traditionally served with Risotto alla Milanese (Milan-Style Risotto, page 164), it's a meal that feels both elegant and homey. The marrow in the bone is a prized delicacy, the kind of detail that Italians get really excited about. Every time Alessio hears "ossobuco," his mouth waters. To be honest, I never understood the obsession … that is, until I tasted it for myself. Now I get what all the hype is about. It deserves all the reverence they give it.

For the gremolata:

Zest of 1 lemon

1 garlic clove, minced

2 tbsp finely chopped fresh parsley

For the ossobuco:

4 veal shanks

⅓ cup (40 g) all-purpose flour

Sea salt and pepper, to taste

2 tbsp extra virgin olive oil, divided

1 large yellow onion, diced

1 cup (240 ml) white wine, divided

6 tbsp unsalted butter

8 cups (2 L) beef broth, divided

1 batch of Risotto alla Milanese (Milan-Style Risotto, page 164), for serving (optional)

1. ***To make the gremolata:*** In a small bowl, combine all the ingredients. Set aside.
2. ***To make the ossobuco:*** Make two small, shallow cuts through the membrane along the outer edge of each veal shank to prevent the meat from curling as it cooks.
3. Place the flour on a plate. Salt and pepper the shanks on both sides and then dredge them in the flour, shaking off the excess. Set aside.
4. Warm 1 tablespoon of olive oil in a large sauté pan over medium-low heat. Add the onion and cook for 4 to 5 minutes, until softened.
5. Add ¼ cup (60 ml) of the white wine. Continue to cook the onions until they're shiny and translucent and the alcohol evaporates, 4 to 6 minutes.
6. Transfer the onions from the pan to a small bowl and set aside.
7. In the same pan, add the remaining tablespoon of olive oil, the butter, and the veal. Increase the heat to high and brown the shanks on each side, 3 to 5 minutes per side.
8. Reduce the heat to medium, add the remaining ¾ cups (180 ml) of the wine and allow to evaporate, 6 to 8 minutes.
9. Add 2 cups (480 ml) of the broth and the onions.
10. Cover, reduce the heat to low, and cook for 30 minutes. Add extra beef broth, if needed, to prevent it from drying out. Turn the veal and cook for another 30 minutes.
11. Turn the veal once more and cook for a final 30 minutes, or until tender.
12. Add more salt and pepper to taste, and serve with the gremolata and Risotto alla Milanese for a traditional meal. (We also love ossobuco with potatoes!)

piatti principali

Pollo Arrosto

Roast Chicken

. . .

4 servings

Is there a more iconic dinner than roast chicken? Every culture seems to have its version, but in Italy, Pollo Arrosto is a beloved staple, deeply tied to weekends, family lunches, and the comforting rhythm of everyday life. It's not uncommon for Italian families to pick up a perfectly roasted chicken from a "rosticceria," a specialty shop dedicated to roast meats. There's often a line of people waiting to take home their own herby, crisp chicken that's been spinning on a classic spit.

Alessio's family does this often. During our visits to Italy, roast chicken makes frequent appearances, alongside Crocchette di Patate (Potato Croquettes, page 148) and a fresh salad. It's a delicious and satisfying meal. This homemade version brings that same herb-scented joy to your own kitchen. A generous rub of butter mixed with rosemary, oregano, thyme, sage, and garlic will roast and fill the air with that classic, welcoming aroma. Simple, but oh so good.

- 1 whole chicken (approximately 2½ lbs/1 kg), giblets removed
- 2 sprigs rosemary
- 1 sprig oregano
- 1 sprig thyme
- 4 or 5 sage leaves
- 6 tbsp unsalted butter, softened
- 2 garlic cloves, minced
- Sea salt and pepper, to taste
- Extra virgin olive oil
- Crocchette di Patate (Potato Croquettes, page 148), for serving (optional)
- Verdure al Forno (Oven-Roasted Vegetables, page 100), for serving (optional)

Special Equipment

- Butcher's twine
- Baking dish or roasting pan
- Meat thermometer

1. Preheat the oven to 350°F (180°C).
2. Truss the chicken using butcher's twine so that it holds its shape in the oven: This involves tying together the ends of the drumsticks, crossing under the bottom, and tying in a knot back over the top of the breast.
3. Remove the stems and finely chop the rosemary, oregano, thyme, and sage.
4. In a small bowl, combine the butter with the herbs, garlic, salt, and pepper to create a paste.
5. Drizzle some olive oil in a baking dish or roasting pan. Place the chicken in the baking dish and massage the herbed butter all over the outside and in the cavity. Make sure to coat evenly. You can also gently massage some under the skin. Drizzle some more olive oil on top of the chicken.
6. Bake the chicken for about 1 hour, or until the internal temperature reads 165°F (74°C) at the thickest part when tested with a meat thermometer. During cooking, occasionally baste the chicken with the juices to prevent it from drying out.
7. Serve hot with Crocchette di Patate (Potato Croquettes, page 148) or Verdure al Forno (Oven-Roasted Vegetables, page 100).

piatti principali

Tagliata di Manzo

Sliced Steak

. . .

2 servings

If Alessio isn't ordering Frico Friulano (Friulian Cheese and Potato Crisp, page 167) as his second course, you can almost guarantee he's ordering Tagliata di Manzo. This dish is such a staple on trattoria menus across Italy that it feels like a given. No matter the region or town, it's always there. In fact, it's almost always prepared in the same way: a beautiful, seared steak, thinly sliced, sitting on top of a bed of arugula and tomatoes. It's simple, but it's the kind of simplicity that comes from deep confidence in the ingredients. This is a theme we see often in Italian cooking. Every bite is in perfect balance: rich and savory meat, bright greens, and the last juicy tomatoes hanging around in late summer/early fall. We make this often when we want to feel like we're dining out in Italy—while sitting in our own kitchen.

1 lb (454 g) boneless ribeye, NY strip, or top sirloin steak, 1 inch (2.5 cm) thick (look for a well-marbled and high-quality cut)

2 tbsp extra virgin olive oil, plus more for serving

Sea salt and pepper, to taste

4 cups (80 g) arugula

1 cup (210 g) cherry tomatoes, halved

Shaved Parmigiano Reggiano, to taste (optional)

Special Equipment

Cast-iron skillet

Meat thermometer

1. Remove the steak from the fridge and allow it to rest at room temperature for 1 hour.
2. Heat a cast-iron or heavy-duty skillet over high heat. You want it hot.
3. Once the pan is hot, rub a bit of olive oil on each side of the meat and lightly salt each side.
4. Reduce the heat to medium-high and place the steak in the hot pan.
5. Cook for 2 to 3 minutes on each side for rare, or 3 to 4 minutes on each side for medium-rare. It's best to check the internal temperature with a meat thermometer for the most accurate cook: 120 to 125°F (50 to 51°C) for rare and 130 to 135°F (54 to 57°C) for medium-rare.
6. Remove the steak from the pan and allow it to rest for 5 to 10 minutes.
7. Meanwhile, arrange the arugula and tomatoes on a plate.
8. After resting, slice the steak into ¼-inch (6 mm) slices and place over the arugula.
9. Sprinkle everything with salt and pepper and add a drizzle of olive oil.
10. Serve with a bit of shaved Parmigiano Reggiano, if desired.

Torta di Mele

Apple Cake

. . .

10 servings

This is one of those humble Italian desserts that surprised me the first time I ordered it in Italy. I thought I was getting something closer to an American apple pie, but what arrived was completely different: soft, golden, barely sweet, with slices of apples visible in the crumb of the cake. It's a dessert that doesn't scream "sugar." Instead, it's subtle, evoking a cozy, autumnal feeling in a light way.

There are countless variations of apple cake. Some people slice the apples, while others dice them into tiny pieces that disappear while baking. We slice ours so there's a little bit of extra texture present in the bite. We keep it simple—served warm, with a dusting of powdered sugar and a cup of coffee or espresso.

2 lbs (907 g) Granny Smith apples (about 4 or 5 apples)
Juice and zest of 1 lemon
2¼ cups (270 g) cake flour
1 tbsp baking powder
2 large eggs, room temperature
1 cup (200 g) granulated sugar
⅛ tsp sea salt
8 tbsp unsalted butter, melted and cooled, plus more for greasing
1½ tsp ground cinnamon
1 tsp vanilla bean paste
⅔ cup (160 ml) whole milk, room temperature
Coarse sanding sugar, for cake pan
Powdered sugar, for dusting (optional)

Special Equipment
Electric mixer
Wooden spoon
9-inch (23 cm) round cake pan

1. Preheat the oven to 350°F (180°C).
2. Wash, peel, and core the apples. Slice them thinly. (The thinner, the better.)
3. Add the apple slices and lemon juice to a large bowl. Mix well to prevent browning.
4. Sift together the cake flour and baking powder in another large bowl.
5. Add the eggs to a medium bowl and whisk lightly. Using an electric mixer, begin to beat on low while adding the granulated sugar little by little.
6. When the mixture starts to get fluffy, add a pinch of salt.
7. Continue mixing until everything is light and fluffy.
8. Add in the butter. Continue to mix on low speed.
9. Add the lemon zest, cinnamon, and vanilla bean paste, and mix on low speed to combine.
10. Finally, add in the flour mixture, ¼ cup (30 g) at a time, mixing on low speed to combine after each addition.
11. Once incorporated, slowly add in the milk, continuing to mix on low.
12. Drain the apple slices from the lemon juice and reserve ten to twelve slices for the bottom of the cake pan. Add the rest to the batter.
13. Use a wooden spoon to gently fold everything together to get batter in between all of the apple slices.
14. Grease a 9-inch (23 cm) round cake pan with butter, and sprinkle coarse sugar into the base. Lay the reserved apple slices on top of the sugar.
15. Spoon the batter into the cake pan and bake for 50 to 55 minutes, until a toothpick inserted into the center comes out clean.
16. Remove from the oven and allow to cool completely before turning out the cake onto a serving dish.
17. Dust with powdered sugar, if desired, and serve.

Mele Cotte

Cooked Apples

. . .

4 servings

Mele Cotte might seem like the simplest recipe in the world, since it's just baked apples with cinnamon and honey, but in Italy, this little dish is like medicine. I remember the first time Alessio made it for me when I was sick. He called it an "iconic Italian remedy," a dish that somehow heals you from the inside out. I didn't expect much, but when he pulled the apples out of the oven and I got a soft, fragrant spoonful, I understood what he was talking about.

You'll find this dish in many Italian homes, especially when someone is under the weather. Personally, I think it deserves a place at the table any time. It's cozy, elegant, and adaptable based on your favorite toppings. Serve warm on a quiet night, tucked under a snuggly blanket. And if you do eat it while you're ill, trust the magic of this revered recipe. You'll feel better in no time.

4 large Honeycrisp apples
Honey, to taste
Ground cinnamon, to taste
Optional additions: ground nutmeg, ground ginger, pine nuts, raisins, chopped walnuts, etc.

1 Preheat the oven to 400°F (200°C).
2 Wash the apples, cut off the tops (reserve for later), and use a small knife to remove as much of the core as possible without cutting through the bottom of the apple.
3 Place the apples in a small baking dish so that they sit up straight and fit snugly. Pour in a small amount of water to just cover the bottom of the dish.
4 Drizzle honey and sprinkle cinnamon in the center of each apple. Add optional additional ingredients as desired.
5 Place the tops back on the apples and bake for 20 to 25 minutes, until the apples are soft when pierced with a knife.
6 Allow to cool slightly before serving.

bevande

Cioccolata Calda

Italian Hot Chocolate

. . .

4 servings

If your idea of hot chocolate comes from a dusty packet stirred into hot water, then Cioccolata Calda is about to change your life. Meet the thick, molten chocolate that's closer in texture to pudding than a beverage. The first time I tried it, I was in awe. It felt like someone had melted down a velvety chocolate bar and poured it into a tiny little cup just for me.

In Italy, you'll find Cioccolata Calda all over the country during the colder months. It's often served with a spoon and a tiny cookie. The French version (chocolat chaud) gets a lot of attention online, but this one? It's an under-the-radar gem that deserves all the love. Don't be surprised if it ruins all other hot chocolates for you forever. (I'd say we're sorry, but we're not.)

2 tsp cornstarch

2 cups (480 ml) plus 1 tbsp whole milk, divided

5 tbsp cocoa powder

4 tbsp granulated sugar

6 to 7 oz (170 to 200 g) good-quality dark chocolate (70%–80%), chopped into small pieces

1. Whisk together the cornstarch and ¼ cup (60 ml) of the milk in a small bowl and set aside.
2. Bring the remaining milk to a boil in a saucepan over high heat and then immediately reduce the heat to low, whisking constantly to prevent the milk from burning.
3. Add the cornstarch mixture, cocoa powder, and sugar, 1 tablespoon at a time. Whisk until smooth.
4. Remove from the heat and add the chocolate, whisking until it's melted and the mixture is smooth and thick.
5. Pour into small cups or mugs to serve.

The Perfect Aperitivo

In Italy, the aperitivo isn't just a pre-dinner snack. It's a sacred ritual. From Milan to Palermo, the hours between work and dinner are carved out for catching up with friends, watching the sunset, and gently "opening the stomach" before the main meal. The drinks flow, the snacks are salty, and the pace is slow.

I'll never forget my first aperitivo with Alessio's friends in Italy. I was still learning the rhythm of Italian culture, and I suddenly found myself in a flurry of cheeses, meats, olives, and crackers—each offered with sincere enthusiasm. "If you liked that, you have to try this!" His friends surrounded me, encouraging me to try every single combination of meat and cracker they could think of. Of course, the prosciutto tasted different on a grissini (page 103) versus a tarallo. Every bite was a test and every combination a revelation. We weren't just snacking. We were connecting. Aperitivo was a ritual of generosity, curiosity, and hospitality like I'd never experienced before.

This is your guide to recreating that experience in your own home. Get ready for the spirit of an Italian aperitivo, shared with friends and filled with laughter.

. . .

The Vibe

Time: Early evening, typically between 5:00pm and 7:30pm.

Setting: A long table or kitchen island filled with bowls of salty snacks and glasses ready to clink. Think balcony, patio, kitchen counter, or backyard table.

Energy: Playful, relaxed, and a little indulgent. This isn't dinner, so don't overthink it. It's about pausing, sipping, and nibbling while chatting with friends, with light music playing in the background. Everyone leans in and reaches over the table, sharing and enjoying the bites.

. . .

A Classic Aperitivo Menu

THE SIPS

- Spritz (Aperol (page 135), Campari, or Hugo versions all apply)
- Prosecco
- Wines (red or white)
- Americano or Negroni (for those with stronger tastes)
- Beer (Peroni is a must)
- Nonalcoholic (Sanbittèr, sodas, sparkling water with lemon)

THE BITES

- Olives, taralli, potato chips, assorted crostini.
- Bruschetta with prosciutto and figs (page 41)
- Salame, mortadella, speck
- Small wedges of Parmigiano Reggiano, aged Pecorino, your other favorites (served with honey and marmalade)
- Grissino (page 103; plain and also wrapped with cured meats) and many types of crackers
- Pickled vegetables and onions
- Assorted nuts
- Caprese with fresh mozzarella and tomatoes
- Tramezzini (small Italian finger sandwiches made with crustless white bread; filling options include cooked prosciutto with mayonnaise, tuna salad, mozzarella and tomato, or egg salad)

The Rule: Nothing too heavy. Just enough to open the appetite and tempt the senses.

Set the Scene

- Set everything out in advance. This is a no-fuss moment. Casual is best; you're not going for perfection here.
- Set the tone with some classic Italian songs, jazz, chill bossa nova, or easy listening.
- Dim the lights and add candles. It starts to get dark early in the fall, so lean into these romantic vibes.
- Remember the little details. Set out some small plates, bowls, tiny forks, and cocktail napkins. Add some small bud vases around the table with flowers.

. . .

Welcome Your Guests

- Always greet guests with a drink: Don't wait. Ask your guests what they want to drink right when they walk in the door. Have something bubbly or bitter on hand.
- Serve a few standout bites and don't stress about variety. Choose your favorite cheese, cured meat, type of cracker, etc. It's fun to have options, but don't get overwhelmed trying to make it all happen. A few perfect pairings go a long way compared to a dozen chaotic ones.

. . .

Savor the Evening

- Don't treat aperitivo like dinner. Keep it light and unfussy. Focus on small bites and finger foods, things that people can eat while standing around or easily balance on their lap.
- Play food matchmaker by introducing your guests to flavor combinations they might not be familiar with. "You like Parmigiano Reggiano? Wait until you try it with a drizzle of local honey." You'll soon have guests snacking on your spread like crazy.
- Aperitivo is all about lingering, catching up with friends, not worrying about when you have to go eat dinner. Remember: Italians often eat dinner at 9:00pm or later! They're not worried about finishing up to catch dinner by 6:00pm.
- Never apologize for simplicity: A lot of people never host because the idea of planning an extravagant dinner party is overwhelming to them. They end up missing out on one of the vital necessities of life: human connection. Aperitivo is meant to be simple. That's the beauty of it. It's a time to gather, and it's less about the food and more about the people.

Inverno

Winter

Purè di Patate

Mashed Potatoes

. . .

4 servings

When Alessio first made me these mashed potatoes, I was totally caught off guard. Not because they tasted strange, but because they were *so* smooth and glossy. I was used to rustic American mashed potatoes that were chunky, matte, and maybe sometimes even a little dry. But these? These were creamy, soft, and almost shiny. More like a rich potato puree you'd find in a fancy restaurant.

I quickly learned that the secret is in the milk. It's warmed separately and then slowly whisked into the potatoes so the starch absorbs it evenly. The result is no lumps or dryness. Just an elegant side dish that still fits on your everyday dining table. Stir in Parmigiano Reggiano if you want a bit of cheesy flavor, but these mashed potatoes truly don't need it!

2 lbs (907 g) medium yellow potatoes
¾ to 1 cup (180 to 240 ml) whole milk
2½ tbsp unsalted butter
Pinch of ground nutmeg
Sea salt, to taste
1 oz (28 g) grated Parmigiano Reggiano (optional)
Freshly cracked black pepper, to taste

Special Equipment
Potato ricer (optional)

1. Clean the potatoes and place them in a large pot. Cover with cold water and set over high heat to boil. Cook until fork tender, 20 to 30 minutes (cooking times will vary depending on the size of the potatoes).
2. Drain the potatoes and allow to cool for just a minute before passing them under cold water. This helps to easily remove the peel. Place the peeled potatoes into a bowl and use a ricer or fork to mash them. Place the potatoes back into the empty cooking pot.
3. Warm the milk in a small saucepan over low heat.
4. When warm, set the pot of potatoes over low heat and gently pour the milk over the potatoes little by little, whisking constantly to combine. The puree should be smooth and silky, not dry or lumpy. Add more milk if needed.
5. Add the butter, nutmeg, and salt. Gently stir until creamy.
6. The mashed potatoes can be served like this, or, if you prefer extra flavor, stir in the grated Parmigiano Reggiano until melted and fully combined.
7. Sprinkle with freshly cracked black pepper. Serve.

Finocchi Gratinati

Fennel au Gratin

. . .

4 servings

I've grown to love fennel because of Italy. When you're there, there's no escaping it. Raw, roasted, braised, you name it. This version is no fuss and has no cream. Instead, the fennel is thinly sliced, topped with every herb you can imagine, and finished with crispy breadcrumbs. It smells like an Italian spice drawer come to life. It's lighter than the creamy Finocchio, Patate, e Besciamella (Fennel and Potato Bake, page 175) you'll find in the fall chapter of this book, but it's just as comforting. Each bite is aromatic and delightfully complex.

2 large fennel bulbs
Extra virgin olive oil
Pinch of dried basil
Pinch of dried oregano
Pinch of dried rosemary
Pinch of dried thyme
Pinch of dried sage
Pinch of garlic powder
Pinch of ginger powder
Sea salt and pepper, to taste
½ cup (60 g) plain dry breadcrumbs
¾ oz (21 g) grated Parmigiano Reggiano
1 to 2 tbsp unsalted butter, cut into small chunks

1. Preheat the oven to 350°F (180°C).
2. Clean the fennel and thinly slice.
3. Add the fennel slices to a medium bowl, drizzle with olive oil, and sprinkle with the dried herbs and seasonings. Gently mix to coat the fennel slices.
4. Place in a single layer on a large parchment-lined baking sheet.
5. Sprinkle with the breadcrumbs and Parmigiano Reggiano.
6. Drizzle again with olive oil and top with the butter pieces. Bake for 40 to 50 minutes, until the fennel is tender when pierced with a knife and the breadcrumb topping is golden brown. Serve warm.

antipasti e contorni

Sformato di Cavolfiori

Cauliflower Flan

. . .

6 servings

Sformato di Cavolfiori is what I like to call Italy's version of the casserole. Vegetable flans, called "sformati," can be found in trattorias and osterias all over Italy. They are extremely versatile. Italians often make them with artichokes, spinach, broccoli, or pumpkin—whatever is in season or left over from that week's vegetables. This particular version with cauliflower and potatoes is a winter staple at our house. The cauliflower keeps the dish delicate, while the potatoes, butter, and cheese are the comfort that we crave in cold months.

For the cauliflower flan:

2 lbs (907 g) fresh cauliflower

Sea salt and pepper, to taste

1 lb (454 g) medium yellow potatoes

2 large eggs

⅛ tsp ground nutmeg

2½ oz (71 g) grated Parmigiano Reggiano

Unsalted butter, for greasing

For the topping:

½ cup (60 g) plain dry breadcrumbs

1 lb (454 g) fresh mozzarella, torn into pieces, divided

1 to 2 tbsp unsalted butter

Extra virgin olive oil

Chopped fresh parsley, to taste

Special Equipment

Potato masher

9 × 13-inch (23 × 33 cm) baking dish

1 *To make the cauliflower flan:* Clean the cauliflower and cut it into even florets.

2 Place two large pots over high heat, fill both with water, and bring to a boil. Once each pot is boiling, add salt.

3 Reduce the heat to medium under one pot, add the cauliflower florets, and cook for about 20 minutes, until softened. Drain and place the florets in a large bowl. Mash them with a potato masher until mostly smooth with no large chunks remaining.

4 Meanwhile, add the potatoes to the other pot and boil for about 20 to 30 minutes, until fork tender.

5 Preheat the oven to 400°F (200°C).

6 When the potatoes are done, drain and rinse them under cold water to help remove the peel. Remove the peel, add to the bowl of cauliflower, and mash together.

7 Add the eggs, salt, pepper, nutmeg, and Parmigiano Reggiano. Stir together until creamy.

8 Grease a 9 × 13-inch (23 × 33 cm) baking dish with butter.

9 *To make the topping:* Sprinkle about one-quarter of the breadcrumbs evenly into the bottom of the dish.

10 Spoon half of the cauliflower mixture into the dish and smooth the top.

11 Cover with half of the mozzarella.

12 Add the remaining cauliflower mixture and top with the remaining mozzarella.

13 Sprinkle with the remaining breadcrumbs, break the butter into pieces and dot across the top, and finish with a drizzle of olive oil. Bake uncovered for 25 to 30 minutes.

14 Broil on high for 2 to 3 minutes to brown the cheese and make it bubbly.

15 Sprinkle with parsley to serve.

antipasti e contorni

Lenticchie Agli Erbe

Herbed Lentils

...

6 servings

This rich and deeply savory side feels subtly festive and is the perfect accompaniment to any holiday meal. The unexpected star here is clove. It gently spices and perfumes the pot, alongside bay leaf and rosemary, and gives a subtle, woodsy warmth to the dish. Lentils have long symbolized abundance in Italy, especially at New Year's, when they're traditionally eaten to bring prosperity. Perhaps it's because they look like little coins.

In our house, however, we eat them all season long, often as a healthy side dish at family gatherings. The browned pancetta gives a rich base flavor that clings to every tender lentil. It's cozy, it's old-world, and it's another example of how Italian cooking isn't about being flashy, but instead about letting a few good ingredients shine.

1 lb (454 g) dry green lentils
1 tbsp extra virgin olive oil, plus more for serving
1 yellow onion, finely diced
4 whole cloves
2 bay leaves
1 sprig fresh rosemary
2 oz (57 g) pancetta, diced
½ cup (120 ml) red wine
6 to 7 cups (1.4 to 1.7 L) vegetable broth
Sea salt and pepper, to taste

1. Wash the lentils well, removing any that are broken and discarding any rocks or debris, and set aside.
2. Warm the olive oil in a large pot over medium-low heat and add the onion, cooking until slightly softened and golden, 3 to 5 minutes.
3. Add the cloves, bay leaves, rosemary, and pancetta. Stir to cook and brown the pancetta, 5 to 6 minutes.
4. Once the pancetta is golden brown, add the lentils into the pot and stir to lightly toast them, 2 to 3 minutes.
5. Add the red wine, stir, and allow the alcohol to evaporate, about 2 minutes.
6. Add 5 cups (1.2 L) of the broth, cover the pot but leave a slight vent, and cook for about 40 minutes to 1 hour (cook time depends on the lentils, so follow the instructions on the package). During the cooking time, stir the lentils occasionally and add broth as needed to continue the cooking.
7. When the lentils are fully cooked and tender, remove the cloves, bay leaves, and rosemary stalk, season the dish with salt and pepper, and finish with a drizzle of olive oil.

antipasti e contorni

Pane Rustico

Rustic Italian Bread

. . .

4 loaves

There's something magical about taking a few simple ingredients and making bread. A shaggy, sticky dough somehow turns into a golden, crackly loaf that goes with just about anything. Pane Rustico is a no-fuss bread with a crisp crust and airy interior. It's meant to grace any meal, be sliced or torn by hand, dipped in olive oil, or used to sop up leftover juices or sauce.

This is not the kind of bread you make for perfection, but rather a loaf that you make for the pleasure of baking, eating, and sharing.

As an everyday bread, you'll find it to be forgiving, useful, and homey. A little time and patience and you'll be making it as a new weekly staple to grace the dinner table. Serve it alongside soup, pile it with prosciutto crudo, or dip it in a good olive oil and enjoy.

1½ cups (180 g) all-purpose flour, plus more for work surface
1½ cups (180 g) Manitoba flour
⅔ tsp (2 g) active dry yeast
1⅓ cups (320 ml) warm water
2 tbsp extra virgin olive oil
1 tbsp honey
1 tsp sea salt

Special Equipment
Wooden spoon
Rolling pin
Small casserole dish

1. In a large bowl, whisk together both flours and the yeast until well combined.
2. Make a small well in the center and inside, add the water, olive oil, and honey. Stir with a wooden spoon to combine and begin creating a dough.
3. Once the dough has formed, turn it out onto a lightly floured surface and make another small well in the center. Add the salt into the well.
4. Knead the dough with your hands, incorporating the salt and strengthening the gluten. It will be sticky, but try not to add too much extra flour. Knead for 5 to 10 minutes. The dough should become slightly smoother, stretchy, and elastic. When you pull a small piece, it should stretch without immediately tearing.
5. Place the dough back into the bowl, cover tightly with plastic wrap, and allow to rest in the fridge for at least 12 hours.
6. When ready to bake, remove the dough from the fridge and punch down the center.
7. Transfer the dough onto a floured surface and gently knead for 5 minutes.
8. Cover the dough with a damp kitchen towel and allow it to rest at room temperature for 1 hour.
9. Divide the dough into four equal parts. Using a rolling pin, gently roll each out into a flat rectangle about ¼ inch (6 mm) thick (with the short end facing you). Then use your fingers to roll the dough up from the bottom edge to the top, into a long cylinder. Repeat for all four loaves.

10 Place the rolls onto baking sheets (two loaves per sheet should be fine) lined with parchment paper, cover with a damp kitchen towel, and allow to rise for a final 45 minutes.

11 After the final rise, preheat the oven to 400°F (200°C) and place a small casserole dish of water on the lowest rack. Sprinkle the loaves with all-purpose flour and use a sharp knife to score down each loaf.

12 Bake for 20 minutes and then remove the casserole dish of water and bake for an additional 10 to 15 minutes, until the loaves are golden brown.

13 Allow the loaves to completely cool on a rack before slicing. Store the bread wrapped in paper or wrapped loosely in a clean kitchen towel and placed in a bread box. It should keep fresh for about 2 days. If you want to store for longer, slice the bread and place inside a sealed freezer bag or container and freeze.

piatti principali

Zuppa Lenticchie

Lentil Soup

. . .

2 servings

On a cold winter's night, you need a soup that will warm you from the inside out. This classic lentil version is earthy, nourishing, and packed with flavor. It's a recovery food, a reset food, and a food that will give you a boost of much-needed energy when the sun sets early. The leeks bring a light sweetness, while the cumin and paprika bring warmth. It's simple and affordable enough to make a double batch, and that's typically what we do so that we can have it again for lunch the next day. If lentils bring prosperity (which is the superstition in Italy), then you should be all set with this soup. Don't forget fresh crusty bread for dipping! It's a must. The Pane Rustico (Rustic Italian Bread, page 204) is a great option.

- 2 leeks
- 1 tbsp extra virgin olive oil, plus more for serving
- 1 garlic clove, minced
- ½ lb (227 g) yellow potatoes, peeled and chopped into small cubes
- 1 cup (210 g) dry brown lentils, rinsed and cleaned
- 4 cups (1 L) vegetable broth
- 2 bay leaves
- ½ tsp ground cumin
- ½ tsp paprika
- 1 cup (210 g) cherry tomatoes, halved
- Sea salt and pepper, to taste
- Crusty bread, for serving

1. Clean and thinly slice the white and light green parts of the leeks.
2. Warm the olive oil in a large stock pot over medium-low heat. Add the leeks and garlic and cook, stirring occasionally, until softened, 5 to 7 minutes.
3. Add the potatoes to the pot and stir to combine.
4. Check the lentils and remove any that are broken or shriveled. Discard any rocks or other debris and add the lentils to the pot, along with the broth, bay leaves, cumin, and paprika. Stir, increase the heat to high, and bring to a boil.
5. Once boiling, reduce the heat to medium-low, cover the pot, and cook for about 30 minutes, stirring occasionally.
6. Add the tomatoes to the pot and continue cooking for an additional 10 to 20 minutes, until the lentils are fully cooked. Go by the package instructions for proper cook time, but when finished, the lentils should be soft but not mushy.
7. Add salt and pepper to taste, and continue to cook on low for 3 to 4 minutes, until the flavors meld and the broth thickens slightly.
8. Serve warm with a drizzle of olive oil and fresh, crusty bread for dipping.

piatti principali

Zuppa di Fagioli

Bean Soup

. . .

4 servings

This rustic soup is as hearty as they come. Packed with three types of beans, loads of vegetables, and a rich tomato broth, it comes together with delicious depth. But don't confuse it with Pasta e Fagioli (Pasta and Beans, page 160). This is a thick, chunky soup that's less a first course and more a full meal all on its own. It's the kind of thing you crave after a long day of cold and gray weather. It almost reminds me of the Southern chili my mom used to make, but without the ground beef. The final drizzle of olive oil is important, so don't skip it. It brings all of the flavors together!

1 cup (180 g) dry cannellini beans
1 cup (180 g) dry kidney beans
1 cup (180 g) dry black-eyed peas
2 bay leaves
2 sprigs fresh rosemary, leaves chopped
2 sprigs fresh thyme, leaves chopped
1 tbsp extra virgin olive oil, plus more for serving
1 yellow onion, diced
1 clove garlic, minced
2 large carrots, chopped
1 celery stalk, chopped
28 oz (794 g) whole peeled San Marzano tomatoes
1 tbsp tomato paste
Sea salt and pepper, to taste
Crusty bread, for serving

Special Equipment

Wooden spoon

1. Cover the cannellini beans, kidney beans, and black-eyed peas with cold water in a large bowl, and soak overnight.
2. Rinse the beans and peas, add them to a large pot of cold water (enough to cover the beans by 2 to 3 inches/5 to 7.5 cm), and bring to a boil over high heat. Reduce to a simmer and cook uncovered for 1 hour, stirring occasionally.
3. Warm the olive oil in a large pot over medium-low heat.
4. Add the onion and cook for 5 to 7 minutes, until softened.
5. Add the garlic and cook for 1 minute, until fragrant.
6. Add the carrots and celery and cook for another 8 to 10 minutes, until softened.
7. Add the tomatoes with their juice and the herb leaves. Discard the remaining sprigs. Stir until well combined.
8. Add the cooked beans with all of the remaining cooking water. If needed, add additional water to thin the soup to your liking. Increase the heat to high, bring to a boil, and then reduce the heat to low.
9. Cover and cook for 1 hour, stirring occasionally. As the tomatoes cook, use the back of a wooden spoon to break them apart.
10. After 1 hour, make sure the beans are fully cooked and soft. Remove and discard the bay leaves and stir in the tomato paste. Add salt and pepper to taste.
11. Serve warm with a drizzle of olive oil and crusty bread.

piatti principali

Tortellini in Brodo

Tortellini in Broth

. . .

4 servings

In Emilia-Romagna, where Parmigiano Reggiano is more valuable than gold and pasta shapes are sacred, there's a dish called Tortellini in Brodo. Tortellini in broth defines the region's culinary heart. Before I met Alessio, I had only ever had tortellini served with red tomato sauce, or worse, *alfredo*. That revelation alone still makes Alessio shudder. But in this part of Italy, tortellini are small, delicate, hand-folded bundles, floating in golden broth like gifts.

The first time I had real, homemade tortellini in broth was at Alessio's grandfather's house. Nonno Lino had prepared a huge spread for lunch and, of course, made the tortellini himself. They were served as a first course before a second course of roasted chicken (raised on their own farm), potatoes, and fresh garden vegetables. The pasta was so tender I almost gasped. When the bowl was set in front of me, I hesitated before reaching for the freshly grated Parmigiano Reggiano, unsure if it would be rude to alter the flavors of something he'd taken such care to make for me. But Nonno Lino, with a mischievous grin, bellowed "Butta!" and plopped a giant spoonful of cheese into my bowl. I learned then that there's no such thing as too much Parmigiano Reggiano when it comes to Tortellini in Brodo. At least at Nonno Lino's house. The meal was perfect, the day unforgettable. This recipe will always remind me of that precious lunch and how something so simple, like broth and pasta, can taste like love and hospitality.

For the broth:

- 8 cups (2 L) water
- 2 large carrots, peeled and chopped into thirds
- 2 celery stalks, chopped into thirds
- 1 white onion, peeled and halved
- Sea salt, to taste

For the filling:

- 1½ tbsp unsalted butter
- 1 oz (28 g) pork loin, cubed
- 1 oz (28 g) mortadella
- 1 oz (28 g) prosciutto crudo
- 1 large egg
- 1 oz (28 g) grated Parmigiano Reggiano, plus more for serving
- Pinch of ground nutmeg

For the pasta:

- 1¼ cups (150 g) 00 flour
- 1 large egg
- 1 large egg yolk
- Extra virgin olive oil

Special Equipment

- Fine-mesh strainer
- Blender or food processor
- Pasta machine or rolling pin

. . .

1. ***To make the broth:*** Add the water, carrots, celery, and onion to a large pot over high heat. Bring to a boil and cook for 1 hour. Add salt to taste. Remove the vegetables (reserve for other uses) and use a fine-mesh strainer to strain the broth into a large bowl.
2. ***To make the filling:*** Melt the butter in a large skillet over medium-low heat. Add the pork loin and cook for about 5 minutes, stirring to rotate the pieces until they are browned.
3. Add the browned pork loin, the mortadella, and prosciutto to a blender or food processor. Blend until smooth.
4. Transfer the filling to a bowl and add in the egg, Parmigiano Reggiano, and nutmeg. Mix well, cover with plastic wrap, and rest in the fridge for 1 hour.
5. ***To make the pasta:*** Place the flour on a flat work surface and make a well in the center.

6 Place the egg and egg yolk in the well, along with a drizzle of olive oil. With a fork, gently begin incorporating the flour around the edge of the well. Continue working until a crumbly dough forms.

7 Knead by hand until a smooth ball of dough forms, with all ingredients evenly combined.

8 Place the dough in a bowl, cover with plastic wrap, and rest for 30 minutes in the fridge.

9 Assemble the tortellini by taking the dough ball out of the fridge and cutting it in half. Cover the half you aren't working with using plastic wrap or a clean, damp kitchen towel to prevent it from drying out.

10 Roll out the dough with a pasta machine (or rolling pin) until it is very thin (about 1 mm).

11 Cut the dough into 1¼-inch (3 cm) squares.

12 Place a small amount of filling in the middle of each. Fold the dough over into a triangle, trying to remove any air around the filling.

13 Seal the edges well (use a bit of water, if needed) and then join the bottom corners of the triangle together to create the classic tortellini shape. Make sure all edges are sealed well.

14 Place the finished tortellini on a floured tray and continue shaping until all ingredients are used up.

15 Bring a large pot of salted water to a boil and cook the tortellini for 2 to 3 minutes.

16 Serve the tortellini in bowls with the broth and a generous amount of grated Parmigiano Reggiano.

piatti principali

Risotto al Gorgonzola

Gorgonzola Risotto

. . .

4 servings

There was a time when I wouldn't go near Gorgonzola. The sharp smell, the blue veins: Just the sight of it gave me pause. But Alessio? He's a Gorgonzola devotee. Anytime it's on the menu, he perks up and his excitement is palpable. It took me more than a decade to finally appreciate its creamy boldness. This risotto is my peace offering to him—a gift of gratitude for opening my eyes to *all* of Italy's special cheeses. Even the more unsightly ones.

This recipe is made with Gorgonzola dolce, a more mild, buttery, sweet sister to the stronger, crumbly Gorgonzola piccante. Rich, snowy white with just the right balance of funky cheesiness and delicate indulgence, it's become a winter favorite. It's the kind of dish you eat slowly, spoonful by spoonful, letting the bite of the cheese tickle your tongue.

4 cups (1 L) vegetable broth
3 tbsp unsalted butter, divided
½ medium white onion, diced
1½ cups (300 g) dry arborio or carnaroli rice
½ cup (120 ml) white wine
Sea salt and pepper, to taste
5 oz (142 g) Gorgonzola dolce
2 oz (57 g) grated Parmigiano Reggiano, plus more for serving
Ground nutmeg, to taste

1. Warm the broth in a large pot over medium heat.
2. Melt half the butter in a large sauté pan over medium-low heat. Add the onion and cook for 5 to 7 minutes, until softened. Remove the onion from the pan and set aside.
3. Add the remaining butter to the pan and then add the rice, stirring to toast until translucent, 2 to 3 minutes.
4. Add the white wine and stir. Allow the alcohol to evaporate.
5. Add a couple ladles of broth to the pan, along with some salt and the cooked onion. Continue to stir occasionally, adding more broth as the rice cooks. It usually takes 16 to 18 minutes for the rice to finish.
6. Once finished, remove the pan from the heat and stir in pieces of the Gorgonzola dolce and Parmigiano Reggiano, little by little. Stir until the cheeses are fully melted and mixed in and the risotto is creamy.
7. Add the pepper and nutmeg and stir.
8. Serve with some more grated Parmigiano Reggiano.

piatti principali

Pasta al Radicchio

Radicchio Pasta

. . .

2 servings

This dish came to life on one of those "What can we make with what we've got?" kinds of nights. No sausage or arborio rice to make a risotto, but plenty of radicchio in the fridge. Boom. Pasta al Radicchio was born. The radicchio gently softens in olive oil, and grated cheeses mellow out its bitterness without masking it. If you can find it, radicchio di Treviso is best here. It's tender, elegant, slightly sweet, and mild, but we typically use the standard radicchio more commonly found in grocery stores. Guess what? It turns out just fine. It's a simple dish, but it looks beautiful and special on the plate. Radicchio still isn't a very commonly used ingredient outside of Italy, but the flavor makes a bold impact. This is the perfect dish for when you need simple preparation but still want to impress.

- 7 oz (200 g) dry long pasta (spaghetti, tagliatelle, linguine, etc.)
- 3 tbsp extra virgin olive oil
- ¼ yellow onion
- 1 garlic clove, minced
- ½ radicchio, thinly sliced
- Sea salt and pepper, to taste
- 1 oz (28 g) finely grated Parmigiano Reggiano
- 1 oz (28 g) finely grated Pecorino Romano
- Fresh parsley or dried red pepper flakes (optional)

1. Bring a large pot of salted water to a boil and cook the pasta according to the package instructions.
2. While the pasta cooks, warm the olive oil in a large sauté pan over medium-low heat.
3. Add the onion and cook for 5 minutes, until softened.
4. Add the garlic and cook for 1 minute, until fragrant.
5. Add the radicchio and cook it down, about 5 minutes.
6. Once the pasta is finished, add about ⅓ to ½ cup (80 to 120 ml) of pasta water to the radicchio and drain the rest.
7. Add the pasta to the sauté pan and season with salt and pepper to taste. Cook and stir for about 2 more minutes, until the ingredients are combined and the sauce is creamy.
8. Plate the pasta and top with Parmigiano Reggiano and Pecorino Romano. You can also add fresh parsley or red pepper flakes for added flavor.

piatti principali

Pasta e Lenticchie

Lentil Pasta

. . .

2 servings

There's something beautifully unpretentious about pasta and lentils. Earthy, filling, and humble, this dish has its roots in cucina povera, the traditional "poor kitchen" of Italy. Cucina povera is the kind of cooking that came out of rural communities that often had to cook with only what was locally available, produced in their own gardens or farms, and seasonal. It's a kind of Italian cooking that emphasizes simple, affordable ingredients while also maximizing flavor in order to get the most out of what you have. In cucina povera, nothing is wasted, and flavor is built from patience rather than a huge list of fancy, extravagant ingredients. In this dish, pancetta adds richness and savoriness, the herbs add a delicate perfume to the pot, and the lentils and ditalini melt into each other to create a comfy, creamy goodness you'll instantly want another bite of.

1 sage leaf
1 sprig rosemary
1 sprig thyme
1 tbsp extra virgin olive oil, plus more for serving
1 large carrot, chopped
1 celery stalk, chopped
½ yellow onion, diced
2 oz (57 g) pancetta, diced
1 small yellow potato, peeled and diced into ¼-inch (6 mm) cubes
¾ cup (160 g) dry brown lentils, rinsed and drained
1 tbsp tomato paste
4¼ oz (127 g) dry ditalini pasta
Sea salt and pepper, to taste

Special Equipment
Butcher's twine

1. Bind the sage, rosemary, and thyme into a small bundle with butcher's twine.
2. Warm the olive oil in a large pan over medium-low heat. Add the carrot, celery, and onion and cook until softened, 7 to 8 minutes.
3. Add the pancetta, stir, and cook until browned, 5 to 6 minutes.
4. Add the potato and stir to mix. Check the lentils and remove any that are broken or shriveled. Discard any rocks or other debris. Add the lentils, enough water to just cover them, and the tomato paste to the pan and stir.
5. Add the herb bundle, cover, and cook for about 30 to 40 minutes, until the lentils and potatoes are tender. Stir occasionally.
6. Add the pasta and salt, and add extra water, if needed, to just cover everything. Continue cooking as instructed by the pasta cook time on the package and until the lentils are soft.
7. Once finished, remove the herb bundle and add salt and pepper to taste.
8. Serve with a drizzle of olive oil.

piatti principali

Orecchiette con Cime di Rapa

Orecchiette Broccoli Rabe

. . .

2 servings

This classic Pugliese dish is proof that simplicity can still pack a punch. Bitter greens, spicy Calabrian chili peppers, savory anchovies, and a crunch of toasted breadcrumbs make a bold, rustic, and satisfying dish. But let's address a particular memory I have with orecchiette ...

The first time I had some from a real Pugliese cook, I nearly chipped a tooth. I was not prepared for *that* level of al dente—the level that the Pugliese pride themselves on. Don't come for us, Puglia, we love you, but we cook ours just a little bit more. Not too soft, not too firm, just enough bite to make things interesting without a trip to the dentist. Want to make this recipe even more delicious? Make homemade orecchiette pasta and you'll really understand why this dish is sacred to our friends down in Puglia.

1½ lbs (680 g) broccoli rabe
⅓ cup (40 g) plain dry breadcrumbs
Extra virgin olive oil
2 anchovies in oil
1 fresh Calabrian chili pepper, diced (can sub with ½ tsp jarred)
1 garlic clove, minced
8½ oz (240 g) fresh orecchiette pasta
Sea salt, to taste

1. Clean the broccoli rabe and remove and discard the outer leaves and central rib. Roughly chop into large pieces and set aside.
2. Toast the breadcrumbs in a bit of olive oil in a large pan over medium-low heat. When toasted, remove from the pan and set aside.
3. In the same pan, warm 1 tablespoon of olive oil. Add the anchovies, Calabrian chili, and garlic, and cook until the anchovies dissolve into a cream, about 2 to 3 minutes. Remove from the heat and set aside.
4. Bring a large pot of salted water to a boil and add the broccoli rabe. Cook for 4 to 5 minutes, until just beginning to soften.
5. Add the orecchiette to the pot and cook until al dente, 2 to 3 minutes.
6. Drain the broccoli rabe and pasta together and add to the pan of anchovies, Calabrian chili, and garlic. Stir and cook over medium-low heat to warm for a couple of minutes. Add salt to taste.
7. Serve warm with the toasted breadcrumbs on top.

piatti principali

Pasta al Forno

Baked Pasta with Broccoli and Pancetta

. . .

4 servings

Creamy, cheesy, bubbly ... three of my favorite adjectives to describe food. This is one of those meals that feels like you're wrapped in a cozy blanket on a cold night. If you know me, you know besciamella is my weakness. Swirl it into anything and I'm an instant fan. It's the base of pure comfort food. This recipe has a little twist, though. Part of the besciamella is blended with broccoli, giving the sauce a pale green color that makes it even more special and sneakily nutritious. Your kids might actually start loving broccoli after this!

Between the velvety sauce, crispy pancetta, and broccoli tucked into every bite, this dish is homey and familiar, like an Italian take on your favorite casserole.

1½ lbs (680 g) broccoli

4 to 4½ cups (1 to 1.1 L) Besciamella sauce (Béchamel Sauce, page 224)

5 oz (142 g) pancetta, diced

12 oz (340 g) dry rigatoni pasta

8 oz (227 g) fontina or provolone, chopped into ½-inch (1.25 cm) cubes

2½ oz (71 g) grated Parmigiano Reggiano, plus more for topping

Special Equipment

Immersion blender

1 Clean the broccoli, remove and discard the leaves, and chop into florets about 1 inch (2.5 cm) or smaller.
2 Bring a pot of water to a boil over high heat, add the broccoli florets, and cook for 5 minutes, until bright green and tender.
3 Drain the broccoli and place half into a large bowl. Add half of the besciamella sauce. Blend together with an immersion blender.
4 Add the pancetta to a small pan over medium-low heat and fry until crispy and golden brown, 5 to 6 minutes. Remove from the heat and set aside.
5 Bring a large pot of salted water to a boil and cook the pasta until al dente according to the package instructions. Drain and set aside.
6 Preheat the oven to 350°F (180°C).
7 Place a ladle or two (⅓ to 1 cup/80 to 240 ml) of the broccoli-besciamella mix into a large casserole dish and spread it on the bottom to prevent sticking.
8 Add the rest of the broccoli-besciamella into the pasta and stir to coat.
9 Begin layering the ingredients into the casserole dish, starting with half of the pasta and then half of the plain besciamella, half of the chopped cheese, half of the Parmigiano Reggiano, half of the pancetta, and half of the reserved broccoli florets.
10 Repeat with the remaining ingredients, layering them in the same order as before. Finish with a little extra grated Parmigiano Reggiano on top for a crispy crust.
11 Bake for 25 minutes. Broil for a couple of minutes at the end for a golden-brown crust.
12 Allow to cool for 10 minutes before serving.

piatti principali

Ragù di Alessio

Alessio's Meat Sauce

. . .

About 12 servings of sauce, enough for one 9 × 13-inch (23 × 33 cm) lasagna plus 4 individual pasta servings

This ragù is the heart of our kitchen. Alessio has spent years perfecting it: tasting, tweaking, simmering—working hard to get it just right. It's rich, deeply flavorful, and endlessly comforting. It's the kind of sauce we always keep on hand, stashed in containers in our freezer for days when we need a little warmth on our plates. It's the first thing we reach for when we get home from a long, overseas flight after visiting Alessio's family. It's what we want to eat when we're feeling down, or when we want to celebrate something. It's perfect for every day and every occasion.

We spoon it over pasta, layer it into lasagna, or swirl it into risotto. It's not just a sauce, it's a tradition in our house. A comforting constant that we reach for again and again. The foundation of so many meals and memories. Every family has a sauce that brings people together around a table. A recipe that gets passed down through the generations. This is ours.

- 2 tbsp extra virgin olive oil
- 1 medium yellow onion, chopped
- 2 garlic cloves, minced
- 3 large carrots, diced (1 white, 1 orange, and 1 purple)
- 2 celery stalks, diced
- 1 lb (454 g) 90% lean ground beef
- 1 tbsp fresh rosemary leaves, chopped
- 1 tsp fresh sage, chopped
- 1 tbsp tomato paste
- ¼ cup (60 ml) white wine
- Three 24½-oz (700 g) jars tomato passata
- Sea salt and black pepper, to taste

Special Equipment

Wooden spoon

1. Heat the olive oil in a large stockpot over low heat. Add the onion and garlic and cook until golden and fragrant, 4 to 5 minutes.
2. Add the carrots and celery and sauté for an additional 10 to 12 minutes, until softened.
3. Add the ground beef, rosemary, and sage. Use a wooden spoon to break the beef into small pieces as it browns, 12 to 15 minutes.
4. Once browned and fully cooked through, add the tomato paste and stir to combine.
5. Add the white wine and simmer, allowing it to evaporate and infuse into the mixture.
6. Stir in the tomato passata and mix everything well. Put a bit of water into each jar, swirl to release any leftover sauce, and pour into the pot.
7. Season with salt and pepper to taste.
8. Cover the pot, leaving space for venting, and reduce the heat to low. Allow to simmer for 2 to 2½ hours, stirring every 20 minutes so the bottom doesn't burn. Add a bit of water as needed if the sauce becomes too thick.
9. Make sure that the carrots and celery are fully cooked and soft. Adjust seasoning as needed.
10. Serve over pasta or use in lasagna, risotto, etc. Freeze leftovers for future meals.

Besciamella

Béchamel Sauce

...

About 4 cups of sauce, enough for one 9 × 13-inch (23 × 33 cm) lasagna or similar dish

When Alessio and I made lasagna together for the first time, he let me in on a little secret I had never heard of. Where he comes from, they don't use ricotta in their lasagna (which I had always thought was a traditional ingredient), they use Besciamella, a creamy white sauce made from butter, flour, and milk. In Italy, you can find it premade in cardboard containers at any grocery store, but here in the US? Nowhere in sight. Seeing that it was so important to him, I decided to take on the challenge myself. I was nervous, but when I whisked that first batch and saw it come together with the perfect texture, a quiet pride spread through me. Alessio's reaction sealed it. One taste and his eyes lit up. I knew I'd nailed it. Since then, we've made homemade Besciamella hundreds of times. Use it in lasagna, pasta pasticciata (another baked Italian pasta dish), or as a base for other creamy or cheesy sauces. You'll understand why it's the secret ingredient you've been missing.

8 tbsp unsalted butter
½ cup (60 g) all-purpose flour
4 cups (1 L) whole milk
Pinch of ground nutmeg
½ tsp sea salt

1. Melt the butter in a large saucepan over low heat.
2. Add the flour and whisk to combine and prevent burning. Continue to cook for about 2 minutes to remove the raw flour taste.
3. Continue to whisk constantly while adding the milk, little by little.
4. Increase the heat to medium and continue whisking until the mixture comes to a soft boil, 2 to 4 minutes.
5. Reduce the heat to low and simmer to thicken. Continue simmering for 15 to 20 minutes, stirring occasionally. Once the mixture begins to thicken, stir in the nutmeg and salt.
6. The sauce is done once the consistency is slightly thick and very creamy. It should coat the back of a spoon but still be pourable.
7. Use in Lasagne di Alessio (Alessio's Lasagna, page 227), as a base for other sauces, etc.

piatti principali

Lasagne di Alessio

Alessio's Lasagna

. . .

6 servings, one 9 × 13-inch (23 × 33 cm) lasagna

The first time Alessio told me that lasagna should never be made with ricotta, I thought he was joking. Actually, he was completely serious. In his words, "It's not lasagna without besciamella." I had grown up with layers of ricotta and marinara, and honestly, most of the time, it was the frozen kind. In Italy, however, the ultimate lasagna is all about rich ragù, silky besciamella, and melty mozzarella. Now, I can't imagine it any other way.

This is the dish we bring out for birthdays, holidays, and any other moment that deserves something extra special. It's the centerpiece of our Christmas dinner, the crown jewel of a family Sunday. It's decadent, but most importantly, it's layered with love. One bite and you'll understand why we can easily finish a full pan in one sitting. Hey, no shame here.

⅔ batch Ragù di Alessio (Alessio's Meat Sauce, page 223)

Two 9-oz (255 g) boxes dry oven-ready lasagna noodles

1 lb (454 g) cherry-sized balls of mozzarella (ciliegine)

1 full batch Besciamella (Béchamel Sauce, page 224)

3½ oz (100 g) finely grated Parmigiano Reggiano

Special Equipment

9 × 13-inch (23 × 33 cm) baking dish

1. Preheat the oven to 350°F (180°C).
2. Spoon a couple ladles of ragù into the bottom of a large 9 × 13-inch (23 × 33 cm) baking dish to prevent sticking.
3. Place a single layer of lasagna noodles on top, breaking them into smaller pieces if needed to fully cover the base.
4. Spoon more ragù on top to fully cover the noodles. Don't leave any noodles dry, as the sauce is what will cook the noodles in the oven. They need plenty of moisture.
5. Take six or seven small mozzarella balls, hand-tear them, and place them on top of the ragù.
6. Next, spoon besciamella in three long ribbons lengthwise across the top. Sprinkle with some Parmigiano Reggiano.
7. Begin the next layer of pasta noodles, ragù, mozzarella balls, besciamella, and Parmigiano Reggiano. Keep making new layers until you end at the top of the baking dish. Each time you add a new layer of noodles, rotate the placement (think horizontal, then vertical, then horizontal, etc.) to prevent gaps. You should make around four or five layers in total. The top layer should finish with a layer of ragù and a generous layer of mozzarella and grated Parmigiano Reggiano. This will give it the perfect crispy and bubbly crust. (See Note.)
8. Cover the lasagna with aluminum foil and bake for 30 minutes.
9. Remove the foil and bake for an additional 10 minutes.
10. If needed, broil on high for 2 to 3 minutes until the crust is golden brown.
11. Allow to rest for 10 to 20 minutes before slicing.

NOTE

If using our besciamella and ragù recipes, you will end up using all of the besciamella, but not all of the ragù is needed. Freeze any leftovers in airtight containers and use on pasta or risotto.

piatti principali

Parmigiana di Verdure Invernali

Winter Vegetable Parmigiana

...

6 servings

If you remember our Parmigiana di Melanzane from the summer chapter (Eggplant Parmigiana, page 126), you could call this its winter sister. It's one of our favorite ways to eat our vegetables when the days grow short and you're longing to turn on the oven to help keep the cold at bay. In the summer, we turn to eggplant, but in the winter, it's all about layering roasted fennel, cauliflower, potatoes, carrots, and beets into a beautiful medley of festive colors. Of course, there's melty cheese, too. Golden, ruby, and ivory, this recipe is like a little stained-glass window in a casserole dish.

1 head cauliflower, cut into ½-inch (1.25 cm) slices

1 large fennel bulb, cut into ½-inch (1.25 cm) slices

3 or 4 large colorful carrots (orange, purple, yellow, etc.), peeled and cut into ¼-inch (6 mm) rounds

1 lb (454 g) yellow potatoes, peeled and cut into ¼-inch (6 mm) rounds

½ lb (227 g) beets, peeled and cut into ¼-inch (6 mm) rounds

Extra virgin olive oil

Sea salt and black pepper, to taste

4 tbsp unsalted butter

3 or 4 sage leaves

1 sprig rosemary

1 garlic clove, minced

1 Savoy cabbage, whole leaves cleaned and separated for layering

12 oz (340 g) fontina, sliced

2 oz (57 g) grated Parmigiano Reggiano

Special Equipment

Fine-mesh sieve

Casserole dish

1 Preheat the oven to 400°F (200°C). Line two baking sheets with parchment paper.

2 Place the sliced cauliflower, fennel, carrots, potatoes, and beets onto the prepared baking sheets, drizzle with olive oil, sprinkle with salt and pepper, and bake for 30 to 40 minutes, until tender when pierced with a knife. Note that some vegetables take longer to soften than others, so use a knife to test for doneness. You may need to bake in batches. When the vegetables are all cooked, set them aside and reduce the oven temperature to 350°F (180°C).

3 Melt the butter in a medium saucepan over low heat. Add the sage, rosemary, and garlic, and stir for 5 to 7 minutes, until the butter turns brown. Strain through a fine-mesh sieve into a small bowl, set the butter aside, and reserve the herbs.

4 Begin layering the roasted vegetables in a large casserole dish. This can be random, doing a mix of vegetables in each layer or using a different type of vegetable on each layer. Top each layer with some cabbage leaves, a few slices of fontina, and some of the grated Parmigiano Reggiano.

5 Continue making layers until you finish the ingredients. Make sure to end with the last of the fontina and Parmigiano Reggiano.

6 Drizzle the herbed butter over the top.

7 Chop the reserved herbs and sprinkle on top with some black pepper.

8 Bake for 35 minutes, and broil for 2 to 3 minutes, if needed, to make the top golden brown.

9 Rest for at least 5 to 10 minutes before serving.

piatti principali

Salmone Croccante

Crisp Salmon Fillets

. . .

4 servings

There's something about salmon that just feels right in the winter. Maybe it's the way the coral-pink color brings brightness to the plate, or maybe it's because it's so often served at festive dinners across Northern and Central Europe. This version is simple but delicious, with a golden crust of breadcrumbs, walnuts, fresh herbs, and lemon zest. It's crunchy and aromatic. Quick enough for a weeknight meal, but elegant enough for company. Serve it with Patate in Padella (Pan-Fried Potatoes, page 39), Asparagi al Forno (Oven-Roasted Asparagus, page 36), or a bright fennel and citrus salad.

4 sprigs fresh thyme
1 tuft fresh dill
1 sprig fresh parsley
1 cup (120 g) plain dry breadcrumbs
½ cup (50 g) walnut halves
Zest of 1 lemon, plus juice for serving
Extra virgin olive oil
Sea salt and white pepper, to taste
2 lbs (907 g) skin-on salmon fillets

Special Equipment
Food processor
Meat thermometer

1. Preheat the oven to 400°F (200°C). Remove the leaves from the stems of the thyme, dill, and parsley.
2. In a food processor, combine the breadcrumbs, walnuts, thyme, dill, parsley, and lemon zest, a drizzle of olive oil, and salt and pepper. Blend into a coarse but even texture.
3. Remove any bones from the salmon fillets and place them on a parchment-lined baking sheet, skin-side down.
4. Cover the fillets with the herbed breadcrumbs, pressing down with your hands. Drizzle with olive oil.
5. Bake for 12 to 15 minutes, until the salmon is cooked through and the topping is golden brown. The color of the fish should be an opaque pink, and it should flake easily with a fork. For moist, flaky salmon, aim for an internal temperature of 125 to 130°F (51 to 54°C), and for well done, aim for a temperature of 145°F (63°C).
6. Serve immediately with a bit of lemon juice squeezed on top.

piatti principali

Arrosto di Vitello

Roast Veal

. . .

4 to 6 servings

In Italy, no holiday table is complete without a roast. Among the many options (pork, lamb, even rabbit) roast veal holds a special place of honor, especially in the North. This dish is often the centerpiece of Christmas or New Year's lunch, symbolizing comfort, abundance, and celebration.

The beauty of Arrosto di Vitello is in its balance. The meat is delicate but rich, infused with festive aromas of rosemary, sage, and white wine. It's traditionally served in slices, topped with the juices from the pan, and nestled on a bed of Purè di Patate (Mashed Potatoes, page 196) or sautéed greens. If you're cooking this outside of the holidays, don't worry. Any quiet Sunday afternoon celebrating family and togetherness will do.

2 lbs (907 g) veal eye of round roast or veal loin roast (see Note)
3 sage leaves
2 bay leaves
1 sprig rosemary
Sea salt and pepper, to taste
3 tbsp unsalted butter
3 tbsp extra virgin olive oil
1 cup (240 ml) white wine
2 to 3 cups (480 to 720 ml) beef broth, divided
1 garlic clove, crushed

Special Equipment
Butcher's twine
Meat thermometer
Fine-mesh sieve

NOTE

If veal is unavailable, you can substitute boneless beef eye or round roast. Because beef is firmer and less delicate than veal, reduce the oven temperature to 325°F (165°C) and roast for 50 to 65 minutes, until a thermometer reads an internal temperature of 145°F (63°C). Keep all other instructions the same.

1. Have your butcher tie up the meat, or, alternatively, you can do it yourself with butcher's twine. It should be tied at 1-to-1½-inch (2.5 to 4 cm) intervals along its length to help hold shape and cook evenly.
2. Preheat the oven to 400°F (200°C). Tie the sage, bay leaves, and rosemary into a small bundle with butcher's twine.
3. Using your hands, rub the meat evenly with salt and pepper.
4. Add the butter and olive oil to a large sauté pan over medium heat. Add the meat and brown it on all sides, spooning the butter and oil over the top, 2 to 3 minutes per side (8 to 12 minutes total). Try not to pierce the meat while flipping.
5. Add the wine to the pan, deglaze, and allow the alcohol to evaporate.
6. Once evaporated, add ½ cup (120 ml) of the broth, the garlic, and the herb bundle. Reduce the heat to low and cook for 2 to 3 minutes, until fragrant.
7. Transfer the meat, herbs, garlic, and juices to a medium baking dish, add an additional 1 cup (240 ml) of broth, and bake for 40 to 50 minutes. Occasionally during the cooking, turn the meat and baste it with the juices. Add more broth, if needed, to prevent everything from drying out. Be mindful of the cooking time, as veal can easily dry out if overcooked. Cook until the internal temperature reaches 145°F (63°C) for medium. It should feel firm with a slight give when pressed, and the juices should run either light pink or clear when pierced with a knife. Rest for 10 to 15 minutes before removing the twine and slicing. Strain the cooking juices with a fine-mesh sieve and serve on the side or drizzled over the sliced roast.

Savoiardi

Ladyfingers

. . .

24 to 28 cookies

These delicate, sponge-like cookies are the foundation for one of Italy's most famous desserts—tiramisù. Everyone loves them when they're covered in coffee, mascarpone, and cocoa, but Savoiardi actually have regal origins. They were first created in the late 15th century for the court of the Duchy of Savoy and were intended to impress a visiting French king. Centuries later, they are still beloved both in and out of Italy for their airy texture and melt-in-your-mouth magic. Though we often use the store-bought version in a pinch, homemade ladyfingers are far superior. Their soft, delicate middles are perfect for soaking up espresso, syrups, and liqueur. Use them to make traditional or strawberry tiramisù or simply dip them in your coffee or hot chocolate for a tantalizing sweet treat.

5 large egg yolks
2 large egg whites
¼ cup (50 g) granulated sugar, divided, plus more for topping
¼ tsp vanilla bean paste
Zest of ½ lemon
¼ cup plus 1 tsp (30 g) cake flour
¼ cup plus 1 tsp (30 g) potato starch
Powdered sugar, for topping

Special Equipment

Electric mixer with a whisk attachment
Piping bag with round ½-inch (1.25 cm) tip

1 Preheat the oven to 375°F (190°C) and line two baking sheets with parchment paper.
2 Separate the egg yolks and egg whites into two medium bowls.
3 Beat the egg whites using the whisk attachment on an electric mixer at low speed to begin forming stiff peaks. When they become foamy, increase the speed to medium-high, and gradually add in half the sugar. Continue whisking until stiff peaks are formed. (Reaching true stiff peaks is vital to the correct texture.)
4 In another medium bowl, whisk together the egg yolks, remaining sugar, vanilla bean paste, and lemon zest. Beat on medium-high speed with an electric mixer or stand mixer for 8 to 10 minutes, until thick, creamy, and light in color.
5 Gently pour the egg yolk mixture into the bowl of whipped egg whites and then sift in the flour and potato starch. Very gently, begin to fold from bottom to top to incorporate. Be very careful here, as you do not want to deflate the air you have created in the eggs. This is crucial.
6 Quickly and gently spoon the batter into the piping bag and begin to pipe smooth strips of dough about 3 to 4 inches (7.5 to 10 cm) long onto the prepared baking sheets. Again, be careful not to deflate the air of the mixture. Make sure to leave space between the cookies, as they will expand when baking.
7 Sprinkle with granulated sugar and dust with powdered sugar.
8 Bake for 10 to 12 minutes. They should be pale and golden rather than brown and should bounce back when lightly pressed with a finger.
9 Allow to cool completely on the baking sheets before removing.

Tiramisù

8 to 10 servings

In a country famous for so many iconic desserts, we will always choose Tiramisù as our favorite. Of course, this is a requirement if you hail from the region where it was (maybe) invented. Alessio and the rest of his region will proudly tell you it hails from Treviso, a town in Friuli, though the people of Veneto might have something to say about that. Either way, they both agree it's delicious and a point of pride and many spirited debates.

The name of the dish translates to "pick me up," which makes perfect sense, because just one bite makes us happy. It's our go-to dessert for Christmas and birthdays, but honestly, we'll find any excuse to make it. The key to getting it right is to not oversaturate the ladyfingers. No one likes a watery, soggy Tiramisù. The cookies should be quickly dipped, not drowned. This isn't supposed to be soup.

This is the classic version, made the traditional way without rum, which often surprises people who've only ever had the boozy kind.

2½ to 3 cups (600 to 720 ml) prepared espresso (see Note)

6 large pasteurized eggs, room temperature

1 lb (454 g) mascarpone

1¼ cups (250 g) granulated sugar, divided

26 to 32 Savoiardi (Ladyfingers, page 235)

Dark chocolate cocoa powder, for dusting

Special Equipment

Electric mixer or stand mixer with a whisk attachment

9 × 13-inch (23 × 33 cm) baking dish

NOTE

We recommend preparing the espresso in a moka pot, using our preferred brands of Illy or Lavazza, for best results.

1 Pour the brewed espresso into a shallow bowl or pan to cool completely.

2 Separate the eggs into two medium bowls: Place the egg yolks in one bowl and the egg whites in another.

3 Add the mascarpone to the bowl with the egg yolks. Beat until the mixture is smooth and creamy.

4 Gradually add half of the sugar to the mascarpone mixture, beating until well combined.

5 Using an electric mixer or stand mixer with a whisk attachment on medium-high speed, whisk the egg whites until soft peaks form. Slowly add the remaining sugar, a little at a time, and continue whisking on medium-high until stiff peaks form.

6 Gently fold the whipped egg whites, a third at a time, into the mascarpone mixture. Be careful not to deflate the air in the mixture.

7 Assemble the tiramisù by spreading a small amount of the filling on the bottom of a 9 × 13-inch (23 × 33 cm) baking dish to prevent sticking.

8 Begin quickly dipping ladyfingers into the cooled espresso and placing them side by side in the dish. Avoid soaking them too long to prevent sogginess; you don't want to add too much liquid to the tiramisù. Only dip for a second or so. Continue until the bottom is covered.

9 Using a spoon, drizzle a small amount of espresso over the ladyfingers if the tops are still dry. Again, be cautious not to oversaturate.

10 Spread half of the remaining filling over the first layer of ladyfingers.

11 For the second layer, rotate the orientation of the dipped ladyfingers so they run in the opposite direction from the first layer. (If your first layer was vertical, this layer should be horizontal.) This ensures even coverage and avoids gaps. Top with the remaining filling.

12 Sift a light layer of cocoa powder over the top of the tiramisù. Use a light hand, as too much cocoa will remain dry even after refrigerating.

13 Cover the dish and refrigerate the tiramisù overnight to set.

Strudel di Mele

Apple Strudel

. . .

10 servings

You might not immediately think of Italy when you hear "apple strudel," but it's actually a beloved dessert in northern regions, especially in Alessio's hometown. He claims his grandmother, Nonna Anna Maria, made the best strudel around, with sweet apples, raisins, walnuts, and of course, cinnamon. It remains one of his most nostalgic treats. In fact, it was often the dessert that his other grandmother, Nonna Carla, would whip out as a treat any time we went to visit her.

It's so beloved in the area that when we visited small mountain towns throughout Northern Friuli, we noticed signs in every bar for "cappuccino e strudel," the perfect mid-morning snack. This recipe is a nod to those cozy mountain cafes and Alessio's childhood memories, where the scent of buttery dough and warm apples meant something special was coming.

For the dough:

1½ cups (180 g) all-purpose flour, plus more for work surface

½ cup (120 ml) lukewarm water

2 tbsp avocado oil

½ tsp sea salt

4 tbsp unsalted butter, melted, for brushing

For the filling:

1 cup (200 g) granulated sugar

½ cup (80 g) finely chopped walnuts

¼ cup (38 g) raisins

1½ tsp ground cinnamon

5 to 6 medium apples, finely chopped (our favorite are Honeycrisp)

Zest of ½ lemon

2 tbsp lemon juice

¼ cup (30 g) plain dry breadcrumbs

For final brushing:

1 tbsp unsalted butter, melted

Powdered sugar, for dusting

Special Equipment

Rolling pin

. . .

1 *To make the dough:* Mix together the flour, water, oil, and salt in a large bowl.

2 Turn the dough out on a lightly floured surface and knead for about 10 minutes. Add a little additional flour if sticky, but be careful not to add too much.

3 Shape the dough into a ball, brush with a bit of the melted butter, cover loosely with plastic wrap, and let rest for 30 minutes.

4 *To make the filling:* Preheat the oven to 375°F (190°C) and line a baking sheet with parchment paper.

5 Combine the sugar, walnuts, raisins, and cinnamon in a small bowl.

6 Place the apple pieces in a large bowl and toss with the lemon zest and juice to prevent browning.

7 Roll out the dough on a floured surface until it's about ⅛ inch (3 mm) thick. Gently place your hands (palms down) under the dough and use your knuckles to begin stretching it by moving your hands apart. Continue until you form a square of about 30 × 30 inches (72 × 72 cm). Trim the edges, if needed, to make them neat.

8 Brush the square of dough with the remaining melted butter.

9 At one end, sprinkle the breadcrumbs in a 3-inch (7.5 cm) strip, but leave a 2-inch (5 cm) empty space around the edge to facilitate the rolling.

10 Add the sugar, walnut, raisin, and cinnamon mixture into the bowl of apples and stir to combine.

11 Spread the apple mixture evenly on top of the breadcrumbs.

12 Roll the dough up like a jelly roll, starting at the end with the apple mixture.

13 Working gently because the dough is thin, roll all the way to the other end until you're left with a long log. You can leave the strudel like this or give it a slight curve, depending on the size of your baking sheet.

14 *To brush for the final time:* Place the strudel seam side down on the prepared baking sheet and tuck the ends under to seal. Brush with the final tablespoon of melted butter.

15 Bake for 35 to 40 minutes, until golden brown.

16 Sprinkle with powdered sugar before slicing and serving.

Crostoli

Fried Carnival Dough

. . .

4 to 6 servings

These were my very first carnival snacks and are forever my favorite. While most people know that Venice is famous for Carnevale (Carnival)—think intricate masks, dramatic costumes, and elaborate balls—what many people don't realize is that smaller towns go all out, too. Each one hosts their own extravagant parades and celebrations. One of the most memorable for me was in Maniago, a town near Alessio's village that's known for its vibrant Carnival spirit.

When I saw it for the first time, I was captivated. There were costumed dancers in the streets, massive, decorated floats, and paper confetti raining down like snow. Alessio, who has always loved Carnival and dressing up in costume, was in his element. Then he brought me a box of fresh Crostoli and waited for my reaction. Delicate, crisp, and dusted in powdered sugar, these treats sent me straight to heaven. We ate the entire box and had to go back for more … and then more again so we could bring some home for Alessio's mom. These airy fried treats are as nostalgic for us as they are irresistible, and now every time we make them, we think of that first Carnival together.

4 cups plus 2 tbsp (500 g) 00 flour, plus more for work surface
¼ cup (50 g) granulated sugar
8 tbsp unsalted butter, softened
Zest of 1 lemon
Pinch of sea salt
2 large eggs, room temperature
3 tbsp (45 ml) white wine
1 tsp vanilla extract
Frying oil
Powdered sugar, for dusting

Special Equipment
Rolling pin
Flute-edged pastry cutter (optional)
Candy or deep-fry thermometer

1. Combine the flour, sugar, butter, lemon zest, and salt in a large bowl.
2. In a small bowl, whisk together the eggs, wine, and vanilla extract.
3. Pour the wet ingredients into the dry ingredients and combine until a loose dough forms.
4. On a floured surface, knead the dough with your hands until fully combined, 5 to 10 minutes.
5. Shape into a ball, cover with plastic wrap, and set in the fridge for 20 to 30 minutes to rest.
6. Remove the dough and divide it into four equal portions.
7. Roll out one portion into a rectangle about ¼ inch (6 mm) thick. Fold the ends into the middle like a letter and roll out again to a rectangle of the same thickness. Repeat the folding process two more times.
8. Finally, roll the dough out to a paper-thin width, as a thin dough is crucial for puffing up when frying.
9. Using a knife or flute-edged pastry cutter, cut out rectangles measuring approximately 5 × 2 inches (13 × 5 cm) and make a small 2-to-3-inch (5 to 7.5 cm) incision in the center of each. stack the dough rectangles on a plate, placing parchment paper between layers to prevent sticking. Repeat for the remaining three dough portions.
10. Heat the oil in a large, deep pot over medium-high heat to 350 to 360°F (180 to 185°C).
11. Fry a few dough rectangles at a time, gently flipping them with a slotted spoon until lightly golden brown and puffed, 1 to 2 minutes each. They should start to puff up quickly as soon as they hit the oil.

12 Once golden, remove them from the oil and drain on paper towels to remove excess oil.

13 Dust with powdered sugar and enjoy.

Frittelle

Carnival Fritters

. . .

About 20 frittelle

If you were to follow the sound of laughter and music echoing through the narrow stone streets of an Italian town in February, you'd likely arrive at Carnival. There, behind a whirl of color, masked revelers, and clouds of confetti, you'd find bakery windows piled high with golden fritters fresh from the fryer. These "frittelle" are light as air and have the faintest hint of citrus and wine.

These street treats are beloved in Veneto and Friuli-Venezia Giulia during Carnival season. They might look like humble dough puffs, but they are crisp on the outside and soft on the inside, and when you see them popping up around town, you know it's time to party. Just like Carnival season itself, they're sweet and fleeting, and you spend the rest of the year dreaming of them.

½ cup (80 g) raisins
1½ cups (360 ml) whole milk
¼ cup (50 g) granulated sugar, plus more for topping
1 tbsp unsalted butter
⅛ tsp sea salt
1½ cups (180 g) all-purpose flour, divided
3 large eggs
1 tsp baking powder
Zest of 1 orange
Zest of 1 lemon
Frying oil

Special Equipment
Candy or deep-fry thermometer

1. In a small bowl, cover the raisins with hot water and soak for 1 hour.
2. Combine the milk, sugar, butter, and salt in a large saucepan over medium-low heat. Whisk and bring to a low boil.
3. Add in 1 cup (120 g) of the flour and mix well with the whisk. Cover and cook, stirring constantly, for 3 to 4 minutes, until smooth.
4. Scrape the batter into a large bowl and let cool for 3 to 4 minutes. Add the eggs, one at a time, stirring in between to incorporate each.
5. Add the remaining ½ cup (60 g) flour and the baking powder and stir to combine.
6. Drain the raisins and dry them with a paper towel. Fold them into the batter, along with the orange and lemon zest.
7. Heat the oil to 350 to 360°F (180 to 185°C) in a deep pot over medium-high heat.
8. Drop 2-inch (5 cm) spoonfuls into the oil and fry, flipping occasionally, until golden brown, 3 to 4 minutes. Fry only a few at a time to keep the oil from becoming overcrowded.
9. Drain on a paper towel–lined plate.
10. While still warm, roll each fritter in additional sugar and enjoy.

bevande

Vin Brulé

Mulled Wine

. . .

About 6 servings

If winter in Italy had a scent, it would be this: red wine simmering with cloves, citrus peel, and cinnamon. Vin Brulé dates back to ancient Rome, where spiced wines were revered for their flavor and supposed health benefits. Today, this cozy drink is a staple at Christmas markets, alpine lodges, and village festivals across Italy.

In Friuli-Venezia Giulia, where this particular version comes from, it's often served by the ladleful in small cups at outdoor holiday gatherings. It's the perfect way to warm yourself up while strolling through glittering piazzas, shopping along snowy streets, or huddled by a bonfire with friends. Sip it slowly and enjoy the deep, festive flavors.

½ cup (100 g) granulated sugar
8 whole cloves
5 juniper berries
2 cinnamon sticks
Zest of 1 lemon
Zest of 1 orange
Ground nutmeg, to taste
Star anise, to taste
4 cups (1 L) red wine (Merlot, Cabernet Sauvignon, or Cabernet Franc)

Special Equipment
Fine-mesh strainer

1 In a large pot over medium heat, add the sugar, cloves, juniper berries, cinnamon sticks, lemon and orange zest, nutmeg, and star anise. Cook for 1 to 2 minutes, stirring constantly, until fragrant.
2 Add the red wine and stir to combine.
3 Increase the heat to high, bring to a boil, and then reduce the heat to low and simmer uncovered for 30 minutes.
4 Strain the wine using a fine-mesh strainer and serve hot in mugs or glasses.

Italian Christmas

In Italy, Christmas is a season-long celebration steeped in tradition, regional pride, and of course, food. Strings of lights shimmer above cobblestone streets, bars overflow with friends clinking glasses of Prosecco, and the smell of spiced vin brulé drifts through the air as people scurry between vendors at Christmas markets. While each region brings its own signature dish to the table, there are a few things that hold true across the country. Meals are long, lingering, and never rushed. Family is everything. Food tells a story. From seafood on Christmas Eve to tortellini in broth on Christmas Day, the table is set for memory-making and celebrating what's special to each individual family.

In the US, our Christmases can seem fast and flashy. In Italy, to rush it would be a sin. Of course, the atmosphere is still festive. People are bustling around the specialty food shops and kitchen for days. However, the table is sacred, and you might find yourself there for hours at a time, pacing between leisurely courses, always saying yes to seconds, and never, ever skipping dessert.

This is your invitation to bring some of that Italian spirit to your own Christmas celebrations.

. . .

The Vibe

Time: Midday on December 25th (Natale, which is "Christmas" in Italian), typically starting around 12:00pm or 1:00pm.

Setting: A long table set with a simple white cloth, greenery, and candles. Less is more, as the food is typically the centerpiece. Bring out your fancy plates, glasses, and napkins.

Energy: Joyful and generous. Time slows down. Music plays softly. There's meat being carved, bread being passed, wineglasses always being refilled. The air smells like citrus, rosemary, and roast. The room is full of laughter, stories, and maybe a little chaos from all of the people gathered together.

. . .

The Menus

CLASSIC PASINI CHRISTMAS MEAL

(Based on our own version we enjoy at home in the US)

Antipasto: Taralli, olives, prosciutto crudo, and chunks of Parmigiano Reggiano

Primo: Lasagne di Alessio (page 227)

Contorno: A simple green salad or crisp radicchio salad with salt, pepper, extra virgin olive oil, and balsamic vinegar

Dolce: Tiramisù (page 236), made the day before so that it's perfectly soft and creamy for Christmas day

Bevande: A glass of Prosecco served with the antipasto, a glass of red wine served with the lasagna, and espresso or Vin Brulé (page 244) after dessert

TRADITIONAL ITALIAN CHRISTMAS LUNCH

Antipasto: Grissini (page 103) wrapped with prosciutto, mortadella with pistachio, fresh ciabatta and olive oil, bruschetta with ricotta and sliced salmon (page 41), olives, vegetables in brine, various cheeses

Primo: Tortellini in Brodo (page 210)

Secondo: Arrosto di Vitello (page 232)

Contorno: Purè di Patate (page 196) or Patate in Padelle (page 39) along with radicchio salad or Spinaci ai Formaggi (page 144)

Dolce: Panettone or pandoro (traditional Italian Christmas cakes), or Torta di Mele (page 186)

Bevande: Prosecco to start, red wine with dinner, espresso after dessert, amaro to finish

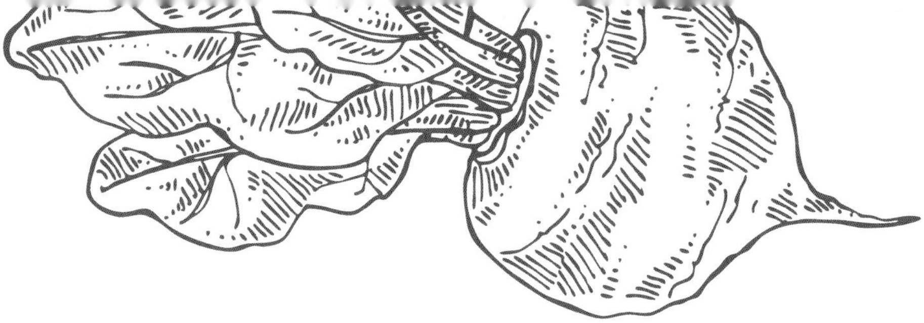

Set the Scene

- Some of your dishes might take time to cook and perfect. For example, tiramisù tastes best the next day, and the perfect ragù for lasagna needs to simmer for a couple of hours.
- Bring out your nice dinnerware: This is the moment for your grandmother's china or your thrifted crystal glasses.
- Light some candles. When it's dark before 5:00pm in the winter, everyone will appreciate the added sparkle and romance.
- Play classic Christmas songs, because Italians love them, too. Believe it or not, they're belting out Bing Crosby all season long.

. . .

Welcome Your Guests

- Lean into festive smells. Fresh herbs or roasted aromas, vin brulé on the stove. Your guests will instantly feel comfortable and nostalgic when they enter your home.
- Serve family style and keep the table full. Let the food be the centerpiece so you can keep decor and tablescapes simple.
- Give little gifts: A traditional gift around the holidays is a pandoro or a panettone. Send each person home with a mini version of the baked cakes and a small bottle of Prosecco.

. . .

Savor the Holiday

- Don't rush the meal. Leave time between courses. Italians leave plenty of time to digest before bringing out the next plate of food.
- Keep dessert simple and casual. Homemade tiramisù served straight from the casserole dish or a store-bought pandoro sliced like a star and served with whipped cream.
- Make new traditions. Blend the old with the new and don't be afraid to let things adapt naturally. It's how the best rituals are born, and it's how we've blended our own two cultures under one roof. Take what you love most and make it work for you and your own family.

Index

D

E

F

G

H

I

J

K

L

M

N

O

P

Q

R

S

T

V

W

Z

Acknowledgments

. . .

First and foremost, we'd like to thank our wonderful families, whose recipes, love, and encouragement we hope can be felt throughout this cookbook. We both grew up in homes where food meant more than just something on a plate, where time spent baking together, the aromas of holiday meals, and recipes passed down as sacred gifts shaped who we are today. We cherish the memories our families have given us, and we hope to continue the tradition of delicious food and togetherness with our own children and grandchildren someday.

To our social media community, thank you for your unending support and for giving us a place to share our recipes, adventures, and lives. For everyone who has followed our journey, cooked one of our dishes, and shared in the laughter and chaos of our kitchen, you are a part of our story. You have given us a huge blessing and created a community that feels like a true family. You've helped us through good times and bad, and we hope the gift of these recipes can bless you and yours.

To our friends and neighbors, thank you for the long aperitivo hours, the wonderful conversations over dinner, for always giving us your honest opinions on our food, and for always bringing warmth and fun to our lives.

To our photography and styling team, these recipes would not have come to life without your talent. You captured not only the beauty of the food, but the energy of the stories that are behind each dish. Thank you for believing in this project and for the enthusiasm you brought to the table while helping us share these recipes with the world. The visuals are everything we could have hoped for.

To the DK team, thank you for encouraging us to create this collection and for guiding us each step of the way. You cheered us on and kept us motivated, all while working unbelievably hard to bring this cookbook to fruition. To everyone who touched a page of this book, or was a part of this process behind the scenes—from the editors, to the designers, the tasters, and the testers—we are forever grateful for your efforts and for helping us craft a hodgepodge pile of handwritten recipes into the beautiful creation we have today.

To our little cat, Micia, lover of all baked goods and gelato, thank you for being our first recipe tester and for always being there in the kitchen with us, dancing to music, keeping us company, and giving us unconditional love.

To our son, Lorenzo, who has reminded us how strong love can be. Thank you for completing our family and bringing a new kind of joy into our lives. This book was written before you arrived, but every story and recipe carried a hope of you within it. We can't wait until you're standing in the kitchen cooking with us one day.

Above all, thank you to God for every door opened, every lesson learned, every blessing given, and every love that carried us through.

Jessi & Alessio

About the Authors

Jessi and Alessio Pasini are an Italian and American couple living in the United States. As an Italian husband, Alessio loves trying crazy foods and snacks from the United States, speaking with his hands, complaining about Americanized Italian food, and being adorably charming and loveable. As his American wife, Jessi enjoys trolling Alessio and filming every second of it. Online, they share relatable videos about their delicious recipes, culture shocks, travel stories, and international relationship. Their goal is to bring laughter, joy, and a knowledge of authentic Italian cuisine to all who follow along.